Collins Incredible Science 4

Meenakshi Atal
Debahuti Das

Components of DigiSuite

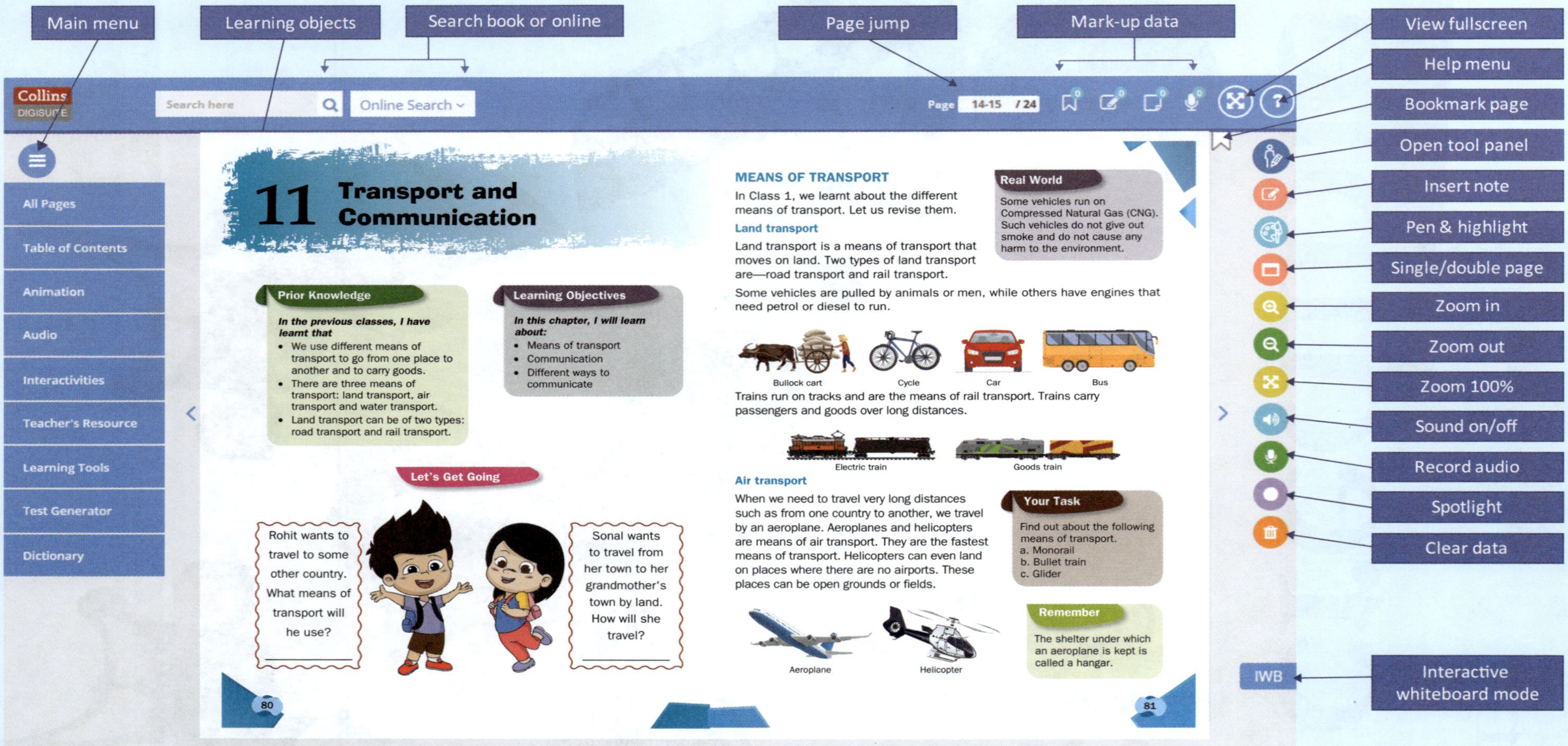

Student + Teacher			Teacher-only	
animations	ia activities	g games	lp lesson plans	tn teacher's notes
ilt instructor-led tutorials	w worksheets	v videos	w worksheets	ak answer keys
	audio			

Preface

Collins *Incredible* is a series of eight books for Classes 1 to 8. **Collins *Incredible Earth 1 and 2*** have been designed considering the multidisciplinary nature of Environmental Studies. **Collins *Incredible Science 3 to 8*** are focused on developing scientific skills and their application in real life.

This series adheres to the guidelines of the *National Education Policy (NEP) 2020* and aligns with the vision of the *National Initiative for Proficiency in Reading with Understanding and Numeracy* (NIPUN Bharat). It adopts the *5E Learning Model* and follows a thematic, coherent and structured approach, effectively integrating subject knowledge, NEP elements such as Experiential Learning, Art Integration, Cross-Curricular and India Focus and *21st Century Skills* for the overall development of the students. The series also aims to make the students aware of the *Sustainable Development Goals* (SDGs) of the United Nations so that they can become SDG Pioneers, Champions or Ambassadors.

***SAFAL* in Collins *Incredible Series*:** This series also strives to make a shift from rote-learning to competency-based learning, in accordance with Structured Assessment For Analyzing Learning (SAFAL). The components of SAFAL—critical thinking, inquiry-based learning and analysis-based learning—are woven into the features such as Skills Enrichment Zone, Worksheets, the latest National Science Olympiad Paper, SEE Learning, Earth/Science Fair and Khagol Talim (Astronomy Education) Worksheets.

We would like to take this opportunity to thank all the teachers, especially Ms Rashmi Ravindernath, who reviewed the books and provided their invaluable feedback.
Any suggestions or constructive criticism from the users are welcome. We shall try to incorporate those in future editions.

Authors

About the Authors

Meenakshi Atal, former Vice Principal of The Heritage School, Kolkata, is an eminent educationist and teacher trainer with over four decades of experience.

Debahuti Das of The Heritage School, Kolkata, has a teaching career extending over two decades and has been a pioneer in evolving innovative methods of teaching.

Key Features

The key features of **Collins Incredible Series** are completely aligned with the *National Education Policy (NEP) 2020* and the vision of the *National Initiative for Proficiency in Reading with Understanding and Numeracy* (NIPUN Bharat). These meticulously designed features, based on the *5E Learning Model*, can be used as learning strategies to help in the overall development of scientific and *21st Century Skills* in students. These key features also aim to help the learners shift from rote-learning to competency-based learning, in accordance with *Structured Assessment For Analyzing Learning* (SAFAL).

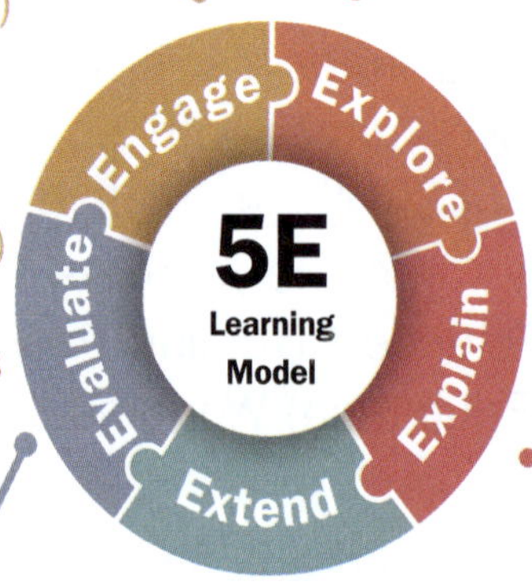

Engage: To capture the attention of students, get them mentally engaged and make connections between past and present

- I Am a Scientist! (Classes 3 to 8)
- Prior knowledge
- Let's Get Going
- Real World
- Science in Action (Classes 3 to 8)
- Concept Map
- Eminent Personalities/Scientists
- Picture Story

Explore: To enable the students to explore the concepts through hands-on activities, investigations, etc.

- Nature Trail/Science Around Us
- Let's Investigate (Classes 6 to 8)
- Tech Updates (Classes 3 to 8)
- Talk About (Classes 1 to 5)
- Your Task
- Let's Try
- SEE Learning
- Earth/Science Fair

Explain: To enable the students to understand the main ideas of the topics

- Learning Objectives
- Remember
- My Dictionary
- Summary
- Keywords (Classes 3 to 8)

Extend: To enable the students to stimulate thinking and apply prior and current knowledge to real-life situations

- Skills Enrichment Zone
- Worksheets

Evaluate: To review, assess and evaluate what students have learned

- Knowledge Check
- Practice Zone
- Review Corner

Adherence to National Education Policy

21st Century Skills (21 CS)

Learning Skills
- Critical Thinking
- Creativity and Innovation
- Collaboration
- Communication

Life Skills
- Flexibility and Adaptability
- Leadership and Responsibility
- Initiative and Self-Direction
- Productivity and Accountability
- Social and Cross-Cultural Interaction

Literacy Skills
- Information Literacy
- Media Literacy
- Technology Literacy

Art Integration (AI)

Cross Curricular (CC)

India Focus (IF)

Happiness Quotient (HQ)

Experiential Learning (EL)

SUSTAINABLE DEVELOPMENT GOALS

Each feature has been tagged with colour-coded icons to easily identify the type of skills and learning being addressed!

About the Features

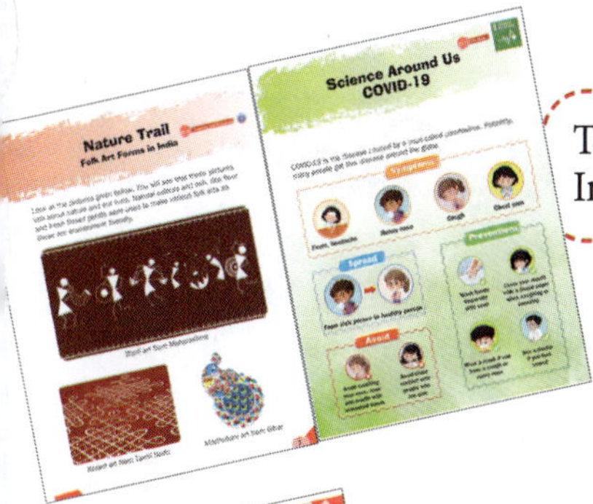

To connect environmental studies/science with Indian history, art, culture and real-life situations

Selective topics that would serve as the basics to becoming a scientist

Interesting project ideas and thought-provoking questions to address the main elements of NEP 2020

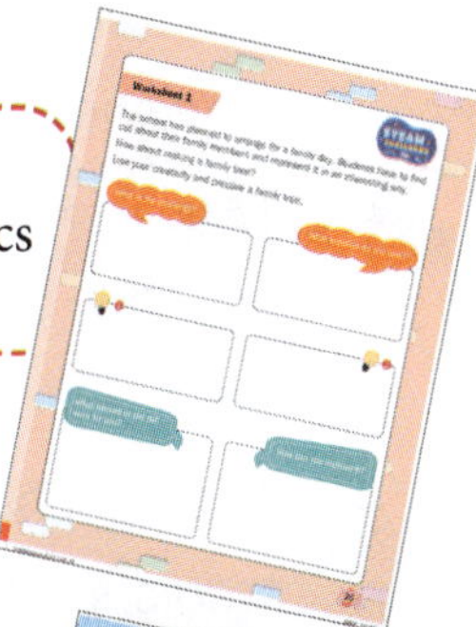

Interesting project ideas integrating Science, Technology, Engineering, Arts and Mathematics to solve real-world problems

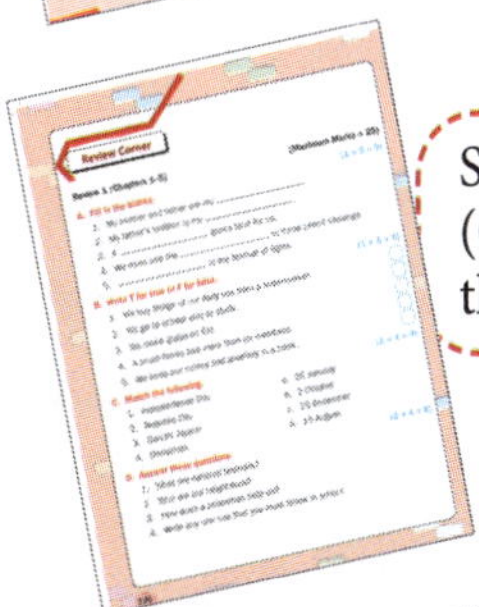

Sample test papers for review and assessment (Classes 6 to 8 Assessment Corner based on the **New Assessment format)**

Colourful cartoon spreads based on environmental awareness

Special stories to promote social, emotional and ethical learning

Innovative projects and model-making ideas that can be displayed in various school events

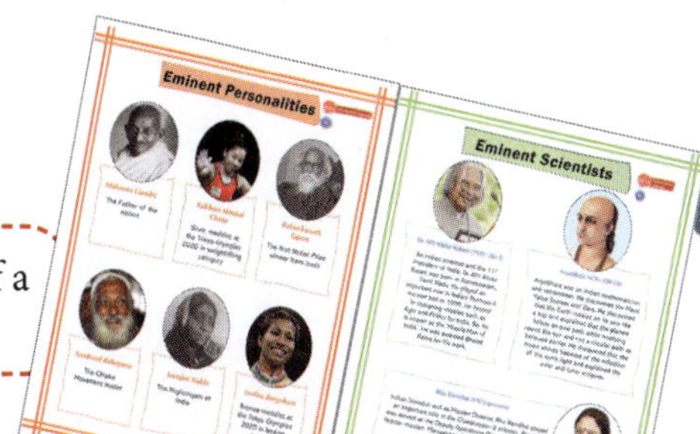

Brief write-up on the contributions of a few eminent personalities/ scientists

Informative and interactive colourful posters to focus on some important concepts or facts

Contents

Science Around Us
Ayurveda

21 CS Information Literacy IF

Ayurveda is an ancient system of medicines. Word Ayurveda is composed of two Sanskrit words *Ayur* meaning 'life' and *Veda* meaning 'to know'. According to this system, good health can be maintained by following a healthy lifestyle that includes practice of yoga, meditation and a particular diet. This system prevents and treats illness by using herbs.

According to Ayurveda, we all are made up of five elements: earth, space, air, water and fire. These elements combine to form three basic qualities or doshas: Vata (space and air), Pitta (fire and water) and Kapha (water and earth).

Every person is made up of a unique balance of Vata, Pitta and Kapha. Hence, Ayurveda suggests a different lifestyle and treatment for every person to stay healthy. A person falls sick when there is an imbalance in the three doshas.

Along with a proper diet, Ayurveda focuses on a healthy lifestyle and routine. According to Ayurveda, some of the healthy habits that help us lead a healthy life are as follows:

- Rising early in the morning
- Starting the day by drinking a glass of water
- Using the bathroom in the morning
- Staying active by practising yoga and other physical activities
- Eating the right food with mindfulness without distractions such as television and mobile screens
- Getting enough sleep

Collect active ingredients such as leaves, flowers, roots, and bark of the medicinal herbs used in Ayurveda easily available in your locality and paste those in the space given below after drying them. If you are unable to find the real samples, search for the images from the Internet and paste here.

Like Ayurveda, there are many other ancient medicinal sciences that are also practised in India and across the world. Search about any one ancient medicinal science and write a brief note on it.

I am a Scientist! (Experiment and Investigation)

21 CS Critical Thinking EL IF

Do you know these scientists?

______________________ ______________________

WHO IS A SCIENTIST?

A scientist is a person who tries to find out how, when and why certain things happen. You are a scientist if you can do the following.

1. Ask questions

2. Make predictions

I think...........

3. Make observations

4. Conduct experiments

5. Draw conclusions

I learnt that...........

6. Report your results

SCIENTIFIC METHODS AND EXPERIMENTS

Science helps us learn about the world around us. We learn to ask the correct questions and find answers to them.

We need to follow correct scientific methods to apply scientific knowledge in real life. Scientific methods help us gather or create new knowledge. It teaches us to learn by doing and finding out.

Real World

Scientists conduct experiments in a room known as laboratory.

Let us now conduct some simple experiments.

Let's Try

Activity 1: Float or sink

Statement: All vegetables float on water

You will need: A potato, a lemon, a coconut, an onion, a carrot and a big bowl of water

Method: Pick each vegetable and predict whether it will float or sink.

Write your prediction in the table. Then, put the vegetables in water one at a time and state what you actually see.

Vegetable	What do you think will happen? (Predict)	What actually happened?
Potato		
Lemon		
Onion		
Coconut		
Carrot		

What did you learn?

Vegetables that float in water ______________________________

Vegetables that sink in water ______________________________

Let's Try

Activity 2: Egg floating

Statement: To find out which egg floats

You will need: Two eggs, water, salt and two tall glasses

Method: Fill both the glasses with water. Add a tablespoon of salt to one of the glasses and stir well. Now drop an egg into each glass carefully and see what happens.

What do you see?

____

____

What did you learn?

Salt water is denser than normal water. The denser the liquid, the easier it is for an object to float on it. So, egg floats on salt water while it sinks in normal water.

____

____

Let's Try

Activity 3: Data collection: Favourite subjects

Statement: To find out which is the most popular subject

What you will do?

Ask your classmates the name of their favourite subject and record the data in the table.

Subject	Number of students
Science	
Social Studies	
Mathematics	
English	

Analysis and conclusion of the recorded data:

- Which is the most popular subject? ______________________
- Which is the least popular subject? ______________________
- What may be the reason? ______________________

____

SCIENTIFIC INSTRUMENTS

Conical flask

Beaker

Test tubes

Microscope

Magnifying glass

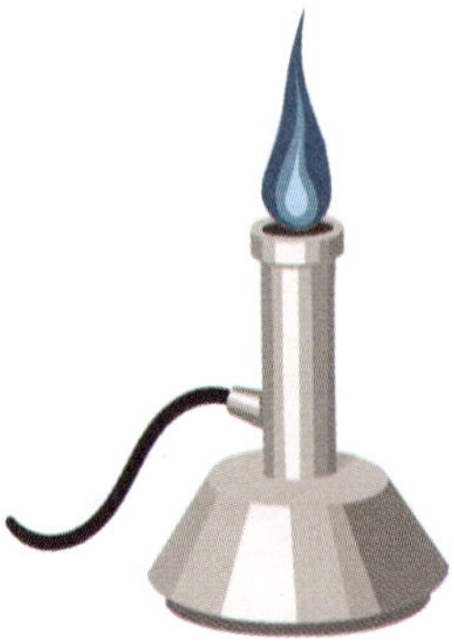

Burner

Your Task

An invention is a new thing that someone creates. Write the names of the inventors of these things.

1. Computer: ____________________
2. Telephone: ____________________
3. Television: ____________________
4. Electric bulb: ____________________

1 The Green Plants

Prior Knowledge

In the previous classes, I have learnt that

- Plants make their own food.
- Leaves are the food factories of plants.
- Photosynthesis takes place in green leaves.

Learning Objectives

In this chapter, I will learn about:

- Leaves
- Green plants make their own food
- Interdependence of plants and animals

Let's Get Going

WHO AM I?

1. I look very beautiful and may have various colours. I help the plant to make seeds.

    ____

2. I support the plant and absorb water from the soil.

    ____

3. I keep the plant upright and transport water to leaves.

    ____

4. I look green and make food for the plant. I am the kitchen of a plant.

    ____

In this chapter, we will learn about the structure and functions of leaves.

LEAVES

A leaf grows from the stem or branch of a plant. The flat part of a leaf is called the leaf blade or lamina. A tube-like structure that runs through the centre of the leaf is called the midrib or main vein. It also has a network of side veins branching off from the main vein. These veins transport water and minerals to and from the leaves. The part that attaches the leaf to the stem or branch of a plant is called a petiole. The outer end of a leaf that is opposite to the petiole is called an apex. The underside of the leaf has tiny openings or pores called stomata (singular: stoma). They allow the exchange of gases. Carbon dioxide enters through the stomata and oxygen from the leaf escapes through them.

Remember

Some leaves have healing properties.

Aloe vera

Tulsi

Parts of a leaf

Your Task

Name any three leaves that we eat.

Real World

Each stoma has bean-shaped structures called guard cells on both the sides to control its opening and closing.

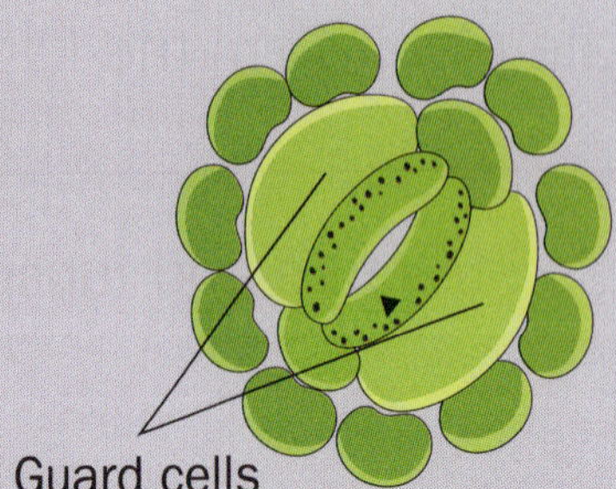

Talk About

Collect leaves from different plants and discuss their shapes, sizes and arrangement of veins.

Real World

Leaves around us!

Different arrangements of leaves

Simple | Compound | Spear shaped

Different shapes of leaves

Round shaped | Palmately lobed

Different edges of leaves

Entire edge | Toothed edge | Lobed edge

Different vein patterns of leaves

Parallel venation | Reticulate (Net-like) venation

Your Task

Make a leaf-print wrapping paper!

Materials required:

- Leaves of different shapes
- Chart paper
- Water-based paint
- Palette
- Brush

Method:

Take different coloured paints on a palette. With a brush, paint the entire surface of the leaf. Press it on the paper. Remove the leaf to find a beautiful impression. Use different leaves and colours to make an attractive wrapping paper!

GREEN PLANTS MAKE THEIR OWN FOOD

In Class 3, we learnt that a leaf is the food factory or kitchen of the plants. Leaves make food for plants by a process called photosynthesis ('photo' means light and 'synthesis' means putting together). The food made by the leaves is sugar. Leaves need sunlight, water, carbon dioxide and chlorophyll to make food for a plant.

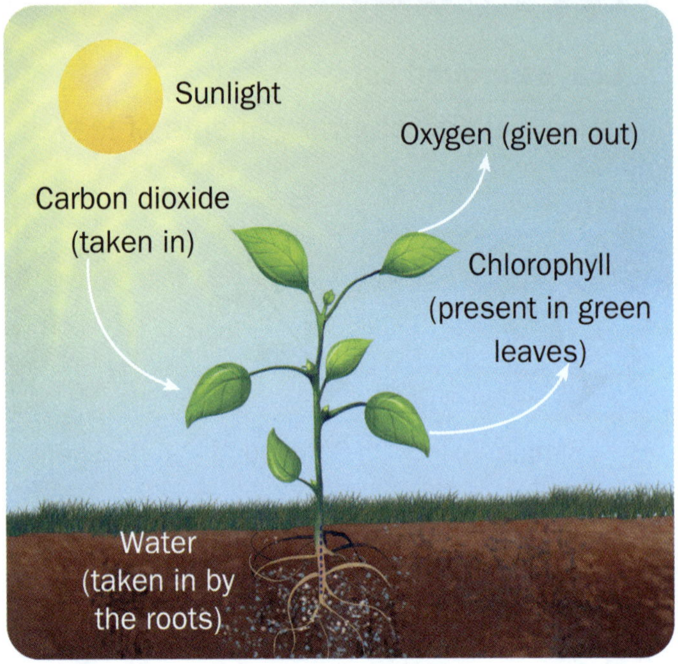

Photosynthesis

Chlorophyll present in green leaves helps them absorb sunlight. They take in carbon dioxide from the air through the stomata. Roots absorb water and minerals from the soil and send them to the leaves. During this process, oxygen is given out by the plants into the air through the stomata. The extra food is stored in roots, stems, leaves and seeds as starch.

$$\underset{\text{(from air)}}{\text{Carbon dioxide}} + \underset{\text{(from soil)}}{\text{Water}} \xrightarrow[\text{Sunlight}]{\text{Chlorophyll}} \text{Sugar} + \text{Oxygen} + \text{Water}$$

Photosynthesis

Chlorophyll traps energy from sunlight.

↓

Leaves take in air through stomata. They absorb carbon dioxide from the air.

↓

Roots absorb water and minerals from the soil and send them up the stem to the leaves.

↓

The food produced is called sugar.

↓

Oxygen is given out through the stomata.

↓

Extra food is stored in the roots, stems and leaves as starch.

Real World

The food made by plants through the process of photosynthesis is sugar and it is used by them for:

- growth and repair
- generating energy to carry out activities such as photosynthesis

Stored food in plants

A cabbage is a leaf that stores starch.

A carrot is a root that stores starch.

A sugarcane is a stem that stores starch.

Let's Try

Aim: To see if the different parts of a plant actually contain starch

Things required: Half a potato, a few drops of iodine, a dropper

Method: Use the dropper to put a few drops of iodine on the flat side of the potato.

What do you see? Write your observation.

____

____

You will observe that the iodine solution gives a blue-black colour to the potato. Thus, we can conclude that potato contains starch.

Knowledge Check

Fill in the blanks.

1. The process by which plants make food is called __________.
2. The tiny holes on leaves are called __________.
3. The food prepared by plants is __________ that is stored as __________.
4. Plants need __________, __________, __________ and __________ to make their food.

Remember

Some plants are parasites. They do not make food on their own and get water, minerals and food from other plants. For example, dodder.

Dodder

INTERDEPENDENCE OF PLANTS AND ANIMALS

Plants and animals depend on each other in many ways.

Green plants make their own food. Plants are eaten by animals. When animals die, their decayed bodies mix with the soil to form humus. Humus gives nutrients to the plants for their growth. When green plants make food, they release oxygen that is used by animals to breathe. Animals breathe out carbon dioxide that plants need for photosynthesis. Animals also help plants in seed dispersal by carrying their seeds to far-off places.

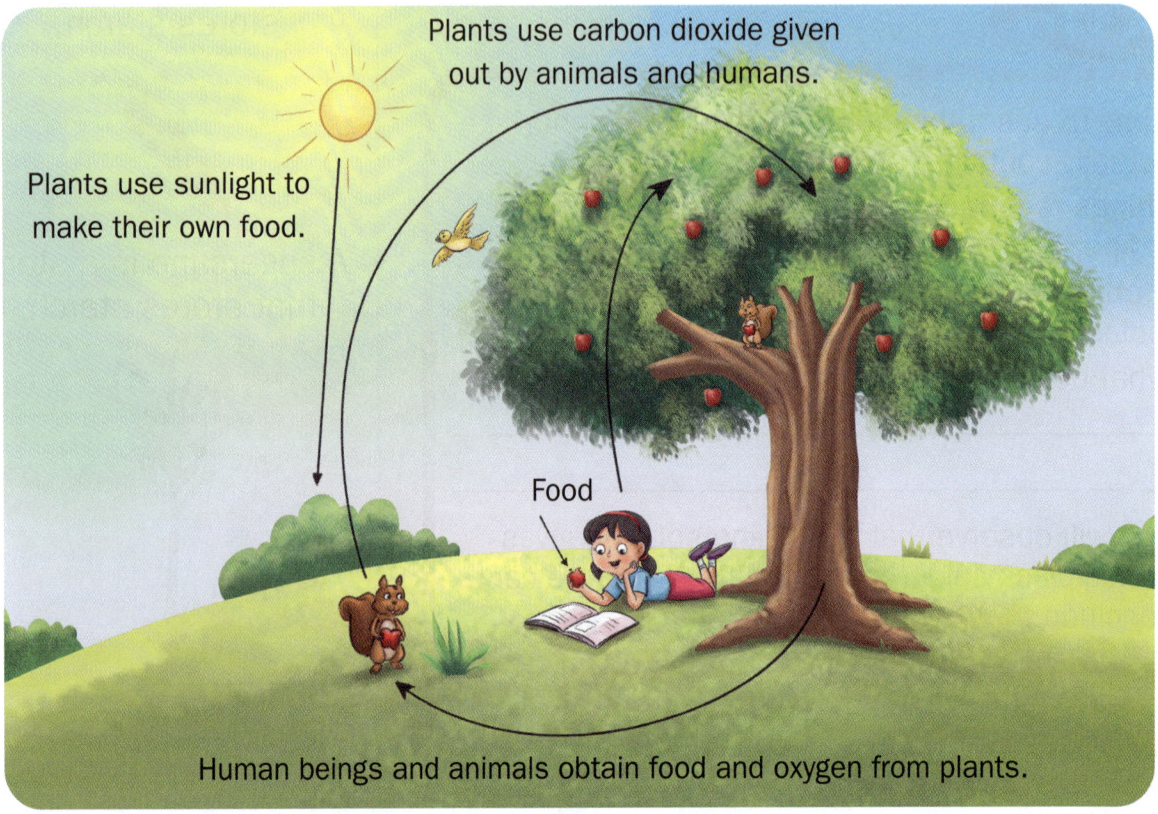

Interdependence of plants and animals

This interdependence between plants and animals maintains a balance in nature. If the number of plants in nature suddenly decreases, the oxygen level will decrease, leading to an increase in the level of carbon dioxide in the atmosphere. Similarly, if the number of animals increases in nature, it will disturb the balance of nature affecting the food chain.

Act Green

Make manure for your kitchen garden by dumping vegetable peels and other green kitchen waste in a pit. Leave the green waste inside the pit for about 2–3 months. Your manure for plants is ready!

Real World

Plants also respire just like animals. They breathe in oxygen and release carbon dioxide during respiration. Rate of respiration in plants is faster during night than day time.

Concept Map

Leaf

- Leaf blade or lamina
- Midrib or main vein
- Side veins
- Petiole
- Apex

Green Plants Make Their Own Food

using

- Sunlight
- Carbon dioxide
- Water
- Chlorophyll

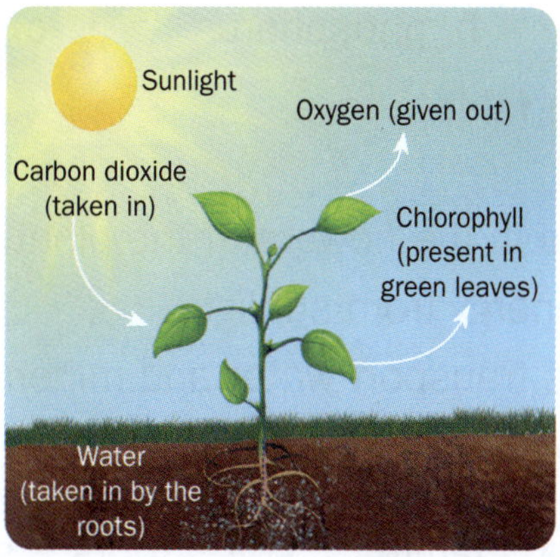

Summary

a. In this chapter, I have learnt that

- The flat part of a leaf is called lamina.
- The part of a leaf that attaches the leaf to the stem or branch of a plant is called petiole.
- The underside of a leaf has openings called stomata through which exchange of gases takes place.
- Leaves use sunlight, water, carbon dioxide and chlorophyll to make food for the plant by a process called photosynthesis.
- The food prepared by plants is sugar and the extra food is stored as starch in the roots, stems, leaves and seeds.
- The interdependence between plants and animals creates a balance in nature.

b. I can do the following:

- Identify the different parts of a plant
- Understand how leaves make food for the plant
- Explain how plants and animals create a balance in nature

Practice ZONE

A. Choose the correct option.

1. ____________ is the part of a leaf.

   a. Midrib b. Petal c. Root hair

2. ____________ allow exchange of gases.

   a. Flowers b. Stomata c. Roots

3. ____________ is stored in roots, stems and seeds.

   a. Oxygen b. Sugar c. Starch

4. When animals die, their decayed bodies mix with soil to form ____________.

   a. humus b. phosphorus c. waste

B. Write T for true or F for false.

1. A carrot is a stem.
2. Extra food is stored in the flowers of the plant.
3. Chlorophyll traps energy from sunlight.
4. The veins of leaves transport water and minerals.

C. Fill in the blanks using the words given in the box.

stem	carbon dioxide	lamina	soil	roots	starch	oxygen

1. Another name for the leaf blade is ____________.
2. A sugarcane is a ____________ that stores ____________.
3. During photosynthesis, ____________ gas is absorbed and ____________ gas is released.
4. Plants get water through their ____________ from the ____________.

D. Give reasons for each of these.

1. Plants cannot make food at night.
2. Some plants are parasitic.
3. Plants and animals are interdependent.

E. Answer these questions in brief.

1. What is the function of stomata?
2. What happens to the extra food prepared by leaves?
3. What is humus? Why is it important?
4. How do plants and animals maintain the balance of oxygen and carbon dioxide in the air?

F. Answer these questions in detail.

1. Draw a leaf and label its parts. Describe each part.
2. How do plants prepare food?
3. How do plants utilize the food they prepare?

G. Out of the box!

We know that plants need sunlight for photosynthesis. How do plants manage to survive during the monsoons when there is no sunshine for long periods of time?

H. Picture Talk

1. Label the diagram.

2. Complete the given flowchart.

Parts of a Leaf

It is the flat part of the leaf.	It is a tube-like structure that runs through the centre of the leaf.	It is the part that attaches the leaf to the stem or branch of a plant.	These are the tiny openings or pores present on the surface of the leaf.

Skills Enrichment ZONE

A. 21 CS Creativity and Innovation | AI | HQ Coexisting with Nature

Make a leaf album!

Collect leaves and put them between sheets of a newspaper or thick books. Remember to change the newspaper every second day. Once they dry up, place them in an album. You could arrange them according to their shapes/size. Do not forget to write their names.

B. 21 CS Creativity and Innovation, Life Skills | AI | HQ Harmony in Relationships

Collect leaves of a peepul tree. Soak them in water till the leaves lose their green matter. Brush out the remains such that only the veins remain like a net. Paste the leaf on a paper to make a greeting card. Give this card to your friend.

C. 21 CS Collaboration , Life Skills | EL | HQ Cooperation and Collaborative Living

Take a potted plant and keep it in the sun. Cover a part of a leaf with black paper for a couple of hours.

Now, pluck the leaf and remove the black paper. With the help of an adult, dip the leaf in boiling water for two minutes, and then dip it in warm alcohol.

Test the leaf for starch with iodine solution as shown in the picture.

What do you see? What can you conclude from your observation?

D. 21 CS Critical Thinking, Creativity and Innovation | HQ How Similar are We | CC Integration with English

15 LIFE ON LAND

Ms Maple Leaf (a leaf on a plant) is making food for her family. Help her write the recipe along with the ingredients and method. Do not forget to mention where she is going to store the extra food.

2 Adaptation in Plants

Prior Knowledge

In the previous classes, I have learnt that

- There are different types of plants.
- Plants grow on land and in water.
- Different parts of a plant have different functions.

Learning Objectives

In this chapter, I will learn about:

- Adaptation
- Classification of plants according to their habitats
- Unusual plants

Let's Get Going

Identify the plants and trees in the pictures and write their names.

ADAPTATION

Different plants grow in different places. The natural home of a plant or an animal is called its **habitat**. The special features that allow a plant or an animal to live in a particular place are called adaptations.

Plants can be classified according to their habitat and the types of leaves, flowers, fruits and seeds they produce.

CLASSIFICATION OF PLANTS ACCORDING TO THEIR HABITATS

Plants that grow on land are called **terrestrial plants**, while those that grow in water are called **aquatic plants**. Plants that grow on dead and decaying matter are called saprophytes and the plants that get their nutrition from other plants are called parasitic plants. Plants that trap and digest insects and small animals to survive are called carnivorous plants.

Terrestrial plants

The plants that grow on landforms such as plains, deserts, coastlines, marshy areas, hillsides and mountains are called terrestrial plants.

Pine tree

Plants in the mountains

Trees growing on the mountains and hilly areas are usually straight and tall. As the mountains and hills get higher, the trees become cone shaped. Here are some features of such trees.

- They have needle-like leaves that are slim and narrow with a waxy covering so that the leaves do not lose much water.
- These trees have a cone shape that allows the snow to slide off.
- They have cones with seeds instead of flowers. That is why they are called coniferous trees.

Pine, fir, cedar, deodar and spruce grow in the mountains.

Plants in the plains

Plains are large areas of almost flat lands. The climate here is moderate and rainfall is sufficient. The trees growing on plains have lots of branches with plenty of leaves and flowers. Some of them shed their leaves in autumn or winter.

Mango tree

- The trees that shed their leaves in autumn are called deciduous trees.
- The trees that do not shed their leaves and remain green throughout the year are called evergreen trees.

Trees such as neem, mango, *sheesham*, *gulmohar*, peepul and banyan grow in the plains.

Plants in the deserts

Deserts have very little or no rain. The plants that grow here have features that help them survive in very dry conditions. Here are some features of such trees.

- They do not have many leaves. Therefore, photosynthesis is carried out in the stem.
- They have fleshy stems as they store water. If you pluck a cactus stem you will find a sticky sap trickling out.
- They modify their leaves into thorns so as to prevent loss of water during **transpiration**.
- They have long roots that spread over a large area below the ground to absorb as much water as they can.

My Dictionary

transpiration: loss of water from the surface of leaves

Cactus

Plants in marshes or swamps

The places where the soil is sticky, clayey and wet are called marshes or swamps. Some parts of such areas may be covered with water. These areas are generally found near lakes, rivers and seas. The plants that grow on marshes are called **mangroves**.

The conditions are difficult for the plants to grow as air cannot reach the roots. Therefore, the plants growing here have roots that grow above the ground. These are called **breathing roots**. They absorb water and minerals for photosynthesis.

Plants in coastal areas

Plants that grow in coastal regions have to adapt to grow in sandy soil, salty water and heavy rainfall. Coconut and palm trees grow well along the coast.

Mangroves

Trees in coastal areas

Aquatic plants

The plants that grow in water are called aquatic plants. Aquatic plants may grow in salt water (oceans and seas) or fresh water (lakes, ponds, rivers and streams).

Aquatic plants are of four types:

1. Floating plants
2. Fixed plants
3. Underwater plants
4. Emergent plants

Talk About

Talk about the different ways you can classify the plants around you.

Knowledge Check

Name the following.

1. Natural home of a plant or an animal ____________
2. A plant that grows on the mountains ____________
3. Trees that shed their leaves in autumn ____________
4. An evergreen tree ____________
5. Plants with breathing roots in marshes ____________

Floating plants

Plants that float on water are called floating plants. Here are some features of such plants.

- They have thick, light, spongy stems filled with air so that they can float.
- They do not have fixed roots. Their roots hang loosely in the water.
- They have stomata on the upper side of the leaves.

Water hyacinth and duckweed are floating plants.

Water hyacinth

Real World

Algae that you see on the surface of lakes and ponds are actually a source of food for many aquatic animals such as turtles.

Fixed plants

Plants that have their roots fixed to the bottom of a pond are called fixed plants. Here are some features of such plants.

Lily

- These plants have long, thin and flexible hollow stems that can sway with the flow of the water and are not torn by its force.
- They have flat, broad leaves so they can float on water.
- They have a waxy coating on their leaves. This prevents them from rotting.
- These plants absorb nutrients from the soil through their roots from the bottom of the pond.

Lotus and water lily are fixed plants.

Underwater plants

Have you seen plants in an aquarium? Where do they grow? Plants that grow under the water are called underwater plants. Here are some features of such plants.

Hydrilla

- These plants grow completely under the water surface.
- They have thin, narrow leaves and flexible stems.
- They do not have stomata on their leaves and hence absorb carbon dioxide and release oxygen directly through their surface.
- They get their nutrients directly from the soil in the waterbed through the roots.
- Tape grass, pondweed and *hydrilla* are underwater aquatic plants.

Remember

Underwater plants support animal life in water as they give out oxygen during photosynthesis.

Emergent plants

Emergent plants are water plants that have their roots in the waterbed but their leaves and stems extend above the water surface.

Bulrush, cattail and arrowhead are emergent plants.

Bulrush

Unusual plants

Non-green plants

The plants that do not have chlorophyll and cannot make their own food are called non-green plants.

Coralroot and Indian pipe are some examples of the non-green plants.

Indian pipe

Saprophytic plants

Plants that cannot make their own food, absorb the nutrients from dead plants or animals are called saprophytic plants.

Mushroom and fungi live on other dead plants.

Mushroom

Your Task

Take a slice of bread or a 'chapati' and sprinkle water on it. Leave it in a box for four days.
What do you notice?

Parasitic plants

Some plants cannot make their own food. These plants grow and feed on other plants for nutrition and are thus called parasitic plants.

Dodder and mistletoe are examples of parasitic plants.

Dodder

Carnivorous plants

Plants that trap and digest insects (and even small animals) to survive in areas with little nutrients are called carnivorous plants.

The Venus Flytrap, pitcher plant and sundew plant trap insects with their special leaves. The leaves digest them in order to get the extra nutrients for their growth.

Venus Flytrap

Concept Map

Types of Plants (Habitat)

- Terrestrial
  - Hills — Example: Pine
  - Plains — Example: Mango
  - Swamp — Example: Mangrove
  - Desert — Example: Cactus
  - Coast — Example: Coconut
- Aquatic
  - Floating — Example: Water hyacinth
  - Fixed — Example: Lotus
  - Underwater — Example: *Hydrilla*
  - Emergent — Example: Bulrush
- Unusual
  - Non-green — Example: Indian pipe
  - Saprophytic — Example: Mushroom
  - Parasitic — Example: Dodder
  - Carnivorous — Example: Venus Flytrap

Summary

a. In this chapter, I have learnt that

- Habitat is the natural home of a plant.
- According to their habitats, plants can be broadly divided into terrestrial and aquatic.
- Deciduous trees shed their leaves in autumn.
- Saprophytes are plants that draw nutrients from dead plants or animals.
- Parasitic plants grow and feed on other plants for nutrition.
- Carnivorous plants trap and digest insects.

b. I can do the following:

- Classify plants according to their habitats
- Explain the characteristics of plants in different habitats
- Connect plant adaptations with the environment

Practice ZONE

A. Choose the correct option.

1. Plants that live in water are called ________________.

   a. terrestrial plants   b. aquatic plants   c. deciduous

2. Mangroves are the plants that grow in ________________.

   a. marshes   b. hills   c. plains

3. ________________ is an example of an emergent plant.

   a. Duckweed   b. Lotus   c. Cattail

4. ________________ plants do not have stomata.

   a. Underwater   b. Fixed   c. Floating

B. Write T for true or F for false.

1. Plants that live on land are called emergent.
2. We can find aquatic plants growing in the ocean.
3. Underwater plants absorb oxygen through stomata in their leaves.
4. Mushroom and fungi are saprophytes.

C. Fill in the blanks using the words given in the box.

thin	saprophytic	breathing	narrow	thorns

1. In desert plants, leaves are modified into ________________.
2. Plants that live on dead, decaying matter are called ________________.
3. Roots that grow above the ground are called ________________.
4. Underwater plants have ________________ and ________________ leaves.

D. Give two examples for each of these.

1. Coniferous trees
2. Plants that grow in coastal areas
3. Floating plants
4. Carnivorous plants

E. Give reasons for each of these.

1. Mangroves have breathing roots.
2. A banyan tree cannot grow in a desert.
3. Some plants eat insects to survive.

F. Answer these questions in brief.

1. What is adaptation?
2. What are terrestrial plants?
3. What conditions do plants living in coastal areas have to adjust to?
4. What features do fixed aquatic plants have?

G. Answer these questions in detail.

1. Describe the plants that grow on hills.
2. What are the features that help desert plants survive?
3. Describe the structure of floating plants.

H. Out of the box!

Deciduous trees in cold countries shed their leaves in autumn to prepare for the winters. When do deciduous trees in India shed their leaves?

I. Picture Talk

1. Where do you think this plant prepares its food?

2. Identify the plants and mention the adaptations they show.

a. 

____

b. 

____

c. 

____

d. 

____

Skills Enrichment ZONE

A. 21 CS Creativity and Innovation, Collaboration | AI | HQ Coexisting with Nature

13 CLIMATE ACTION | 15 LIFE ON LAND

Make a hanging garden!

Take plastic bottles. With the help of an adult, cut the top of the bottles. Fill them with soil. Sow seeds of different kinds in these bottles. You can also colour the bottles and make your favourite animal or cartoon faces. Hang the bottles from a rod. Water the soil daily and see your plants grow!

B. 21 CS Communication | CC Integration with English | IF

Enrich your vocabulary with plants. Find out the meanings of these phrases. Also, write similar phrases in your mother tongue.

1. Green-fingered
2. A rolling stone gathers no moss
3. As fresh as a daisy
4. Like two peas in a pod
5. As tall as a tree
6. Turning over a new leaf

C. 21 CS Creativity and Innovation, Life Skills | CC Integration with Mathematics | HQ Happiness My Goal

3 GOOD HEALTH AND WELL-BEING

Mint cooler on a hot day!

Ingredients:

- One lime
- Sugar
- A pinch of black salt
- Mint leaves (*Pudina*)

Method:

Squeeze the lime into a glass of water. Add two teaspoons of sugar, a pinch of salt and crushed mint leaves. Stir well. Add ice if you want to. Decorate with some lime slices.

Your Mint Cooler is ready!

Worksheet 1

STEAM CHALLENGE

Students of Class 4 went on an excursion to Rajasthan. They saw very little vegetation in some places. The teacher told that due to very little rainfall not many varieties of plants can grow in Rajasthan. Some students asked, "Can plants live and grow when 'watered' with fruit juice, soda or milk?".

Can you design an experiment to show how plants behave when instead of water they are watered with liquids such as fruit juice, soda or milk?

What is the challenge?

What supplies do you need?

1

2

What worked or did not work for you?

How can you improve it?

3 Reproduction in Animals

Prior Knowledge

In the previous classes, I have learnt that

- Living things produce their own kind.
- Some living things give birth to young ones.
- Some living things lay eggs.

Learning Objectives

In this chapter, I will learn about:

- Reproduction
- Animals that give birth to young ones
- Animals that lay eggs

Let's Get Going

Look at these pictures and circle the animals that lay eggs.

REPRODUCTION

Animals are classified into different groups based on their characteristics.

One of the characteristics of animals is that they produce young ones of their own kind. This process is called **reproduction**. Animals reproduce in two ways—by giving birth to young ones or by laying eggs from which the young ones hatch out.

ANIMALS THAT GIVE BIRTH TO YOUNG ONES

Animals that give birth to the young ones are called **mammals**. The young ones of these animals grow inside the mother's body before they are born. Once born, the young ones are looked after by their parents.

Real World

Mammals are also called viviparous animals which means giving birth to the young ones.

Mammals that live on land are called **terrestrial mammals**. Human beings, lions, cats, tigers, giraffes, sheep and cows are some examples of terrestrial mammals.

Mother with her child

Lion with its cub

Giraffe with its calf

Mammals that live in water are called **aquatic mammals**. Dolphins, whales and seals are some examples of aquatic mammals.

Whale with its calf

Remember

Though spiny anteater and duck-billed platypus are mammals, they do not give birth to young ones. They lay eggs from which the young ones are hatched.

Spiny anteater

Duck-billed platypus

Mammals that can fly are called **aerial** or **flying mammals**. Bats are the only flying mammals.

Your Task

Which is the largest mammal in the world?

Bat with its pup

Here are some features of mammals.

1. They give birth to the young ones.
2. They have hair or fur on their body, except dolphins and whales.
3. They **suckle** their young ones.
4. They are warm-blooded, which means their body temperature does not change with the change in temperature outside.

My Dictionary

suckle: a mother feeding the young ones with her own milk

Real World

Animals such as kangaroos have a pouch to carry their babies. Such animals are called marsupials.

ANIMALS THAT LAY EGGS

Birds, fish, insects such as butterflies, reptiles such as lizards and amphibians such as frogs lay eggs.
Their young ones slowly hatch out of their eggs.

The different stages of development, from beginning to the end of life, form a life cycle.

Pigeon with eggs

Life cycle of birds

All birds have similar life cycles. They lay eggs in their nests and **incubate** them. The baby bird develops inside the egg. When it is fully developed, the baby bird pecks open the shell of the egg and emerges from it. This is called **hatching**. The parent birds feed their young ones and take care of them until they are able to look after themselves.

Life cycle of a hen

My Dictionary

incubate: (of a bird) to sit on eggs for weeks to keep them warm till they hatch

This is what the inside of an egg looks like!

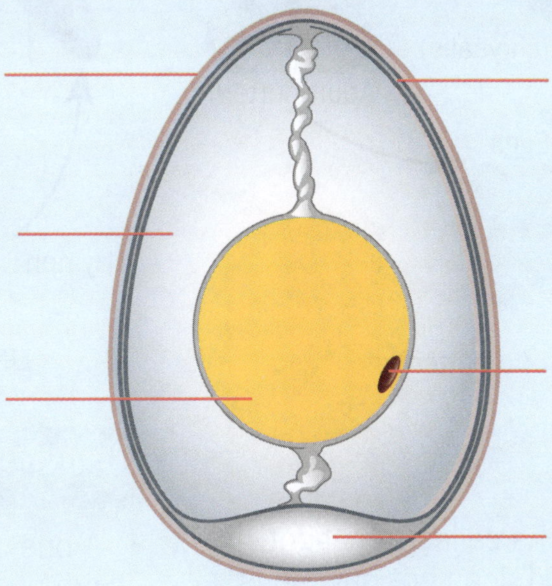

Structure of an egg

Life cycle of insects

For most insects, life begins as an egg. The female lays eggs and leaves them to hatch on their own. The **hatchlings** then go through the rest of the stages of the life cycle. Some insects such as butterflies, houseflies and beetles have four stages in their life cycle, while some insects such as cockroaches and grasshoppers have only three.

My Dictionary

- **hatchlings:** young animals that have newly emerged from eggs
- **moulting:** animals shedding their old skin to develop new ones

Life cycle of a butterfly

A butterfly has four stages in its life cycle. A female butterfly lays its eggs on leaves. A larva called **caterpillar** hatches from the eggs. It grows in size by eating leaves and undergoes **moulting** several times before changing into a **pupa**. When fully developed, the adult butterfly breaks the pupa casing called **cocoon** and comes out.

Life cycle of a cockroach

The life cycle of cockroach involves three stages: egg, nymph and adult.

Nymphs are tiny larvae that hatch from eggs. They closely resemble their parents but do not have wings. A nymph undergoes moulting several times before it grows into an adult.

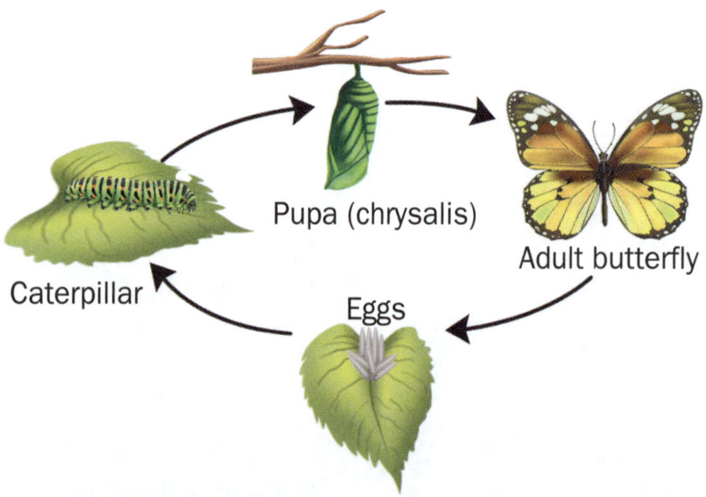

Life cycle of a butterfly

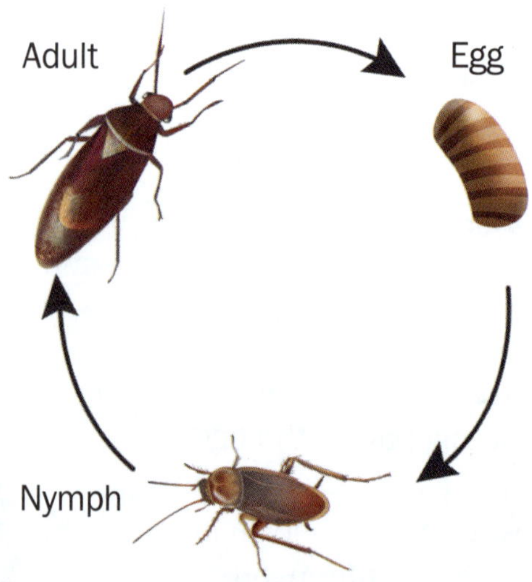

Life cycle of a cockroach

Real World

- The larva of a housefly is called a maggot. It looks like a worm and does not have legs and wings like an adult housefly.
- The Tilapia fish carries its eggs in its mouth till they hatch.

Remember

- A one-day-old cockroach can run as fast as its parents.
- A cockroach can live for about a week without its head.

Knowledge Check

Label the four stages of the life cycle of a housefly.

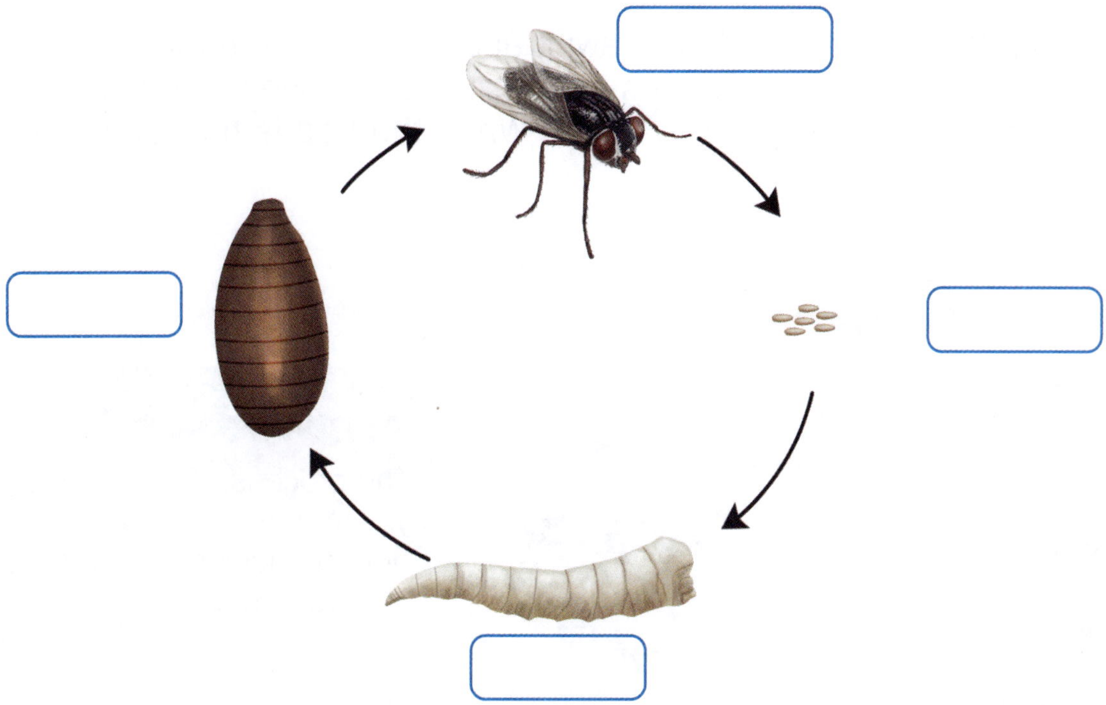

Life cycle of a fish

A fish lays thousands of eggs at a time in water. Many of these eggs are eaten up by bigger fish. The surviving eggs hatch. The young ones called fry are very similar to the adults.

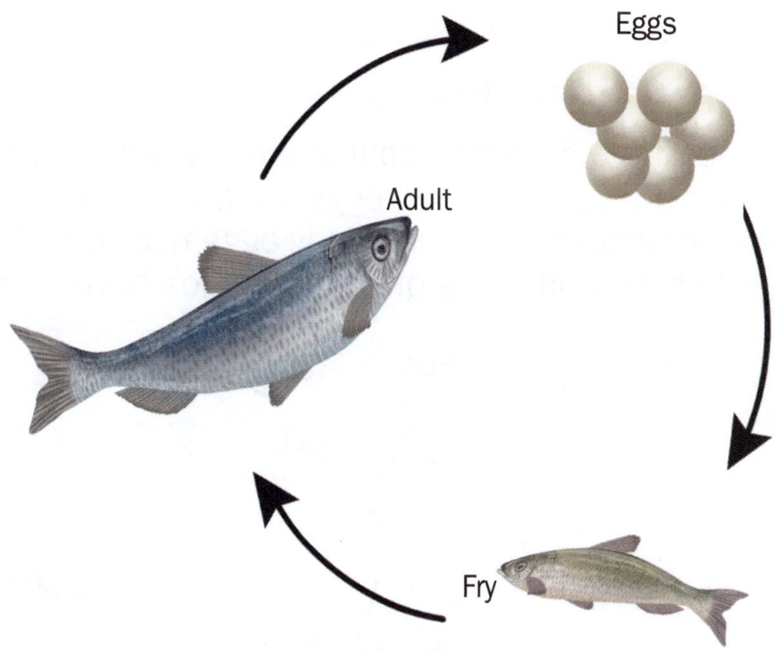

Life cycle of a fish

Remember

No new scales are added to a fish's body as it grows.

Life cycle of amphibians

Amphibians such as frogs lay eggs in water. The eggs appear as large clusters of jelly-like substance called spawn. When the eggs hatch, baby frogs called tadpoles emerge, which do not look like an adult frog.

The tiny tadpoles have a long tail to swim and gills to breathe in water. As a tadpole grows, its tail becomes shorter till it disappears. Its gills become smaller and are slowly replaced by lungs. When the frog is fully developed, it moves on to land.

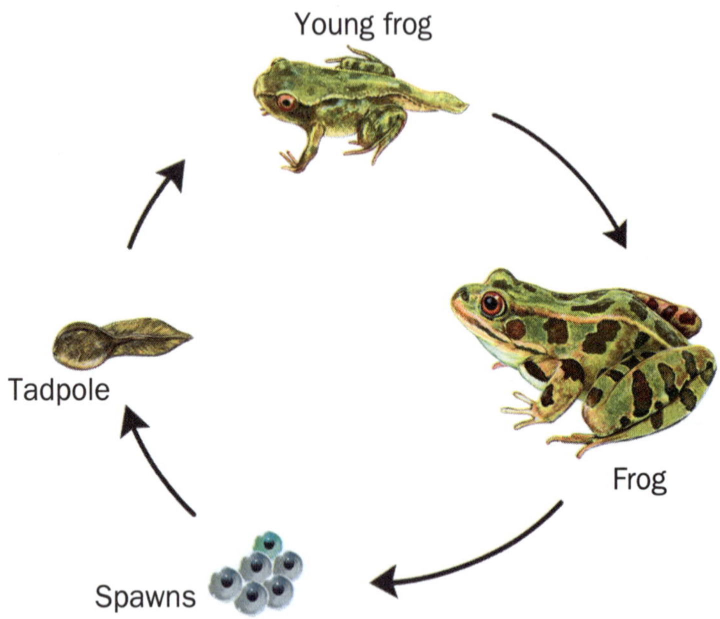

Life cycle of a frog

Real World

The process of changing of a young one into a completely different looking adult is called metamorphosis.

Life cycle of reptiles

Some of the common reptiles are snakes, lizards, crocodiles, tortoises and turtles. Most reptiles lay eggs on land. Snakes lay eggs in a hole in the ground, while crocodiles and turtles lay eggs near river banks. Eggs of some reptiles have hard shells and those of some reptiles have soft shells.

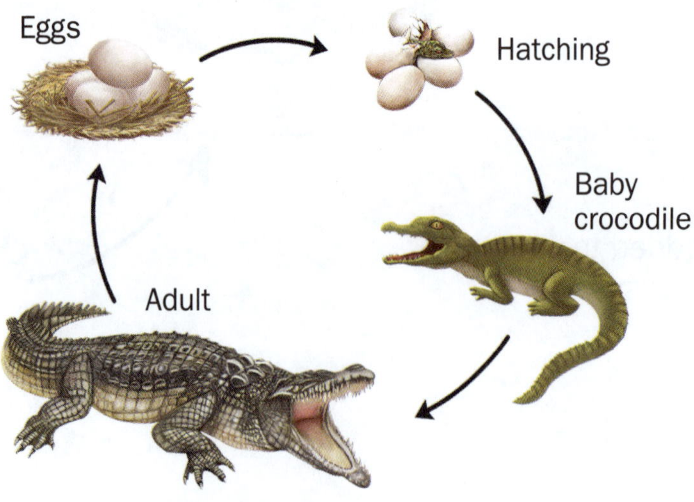

Life cycle of a crocodile

Concept Map

Animal Reproduction

by

- Giving birth to the young ones
  - examples: Mammals (terrestrial, aquatic and aerial)

Lion with its cub

Whale with its calf

Bat with its pup

- Laying eggs
  - examples: Fish, reptiles, insects, amphibians, birds

Hen

Cockroach

Fish

Frog

Crocodile

Summary

a. In this chapter, I have learnt that

- Reproduction is a process by which animals produce young ones of their own kinds.
- Animals reproduce either by giving birth to young ones or by laying eggs.
- Mammals give birth to their young ones.
- Birds, frog, fish, insects and reptiles lay eggs.
- An egg has a hard outer covering called an egg shell, a yellow portion called the yolk, and a white watery substance called the albumen and the developing baby called the embryo.
- Insects go through three or four stages in their life cycle.

b. I can do the following:

- Define reproduction
- Explain the two types of reproduction in animals
- Identify the stages in the life cycle of different creatures

Practice ZONE

A. Choose the correct option.

1. ______________ is an aquatic mammal.
   a. Whale   b. Sheep   c. Bat
2. ______________ is a marsupial.
   a. Cow   b. Kangaroo   c. Anteater
3. ______________ of the egg is the developing baby.
   a. Albumen   b. Yolk   c. Embryo
4. ______________ is a stage in the cockroach's life cycle.
   a. Nymph   b. Larva   c. Pupa

B. Write T for true or F for false.

1. Animals that give birth to young ones are called mammals.
2. The albumen of an egg has air that helps the embryo to breathe.
3. A cockroach has a three-stage life cycle.
4. Tadpoles breathe through lungs.

C. Fill in the blanks using the words given in the box.

spawn	tadpoles	pupa	bats

1. ______________ are the only flying mammals.
2. A larva of an insect develops into a ______________.
3. Eggs of frogs are known as ______________.
4. Baby frogs are called ______________.

D. Give two examples for each of these.

1. Mammals that lay eggs
2. Insects that have a four-stage life cycle
3. Insects that have a three-stage life cycle
4. Reptiles

E. Give reasons for each of these.

1. A bat is considered to be a mammal.
2. A tadpole is different from a young frog.
3. Adult frogs move on to land.

F. Answer these questions in brief.

1. What is reproduction? What are the two ways in which animals reproduce?
2. What do you mean by life cycle?

3. What is hatching?
4. What are the changes that transform a tadpole into a frog?

G. Answer these questions in detail.

1. What are the features of a mammal?
2. With a labelled diagram, explain the four-stage life cycle of a butterfly.

H. Out of the box!

Almost all mammals and birds take care of their young ones. There is one bird that does not. It lays its eggs in another bird's nest. Find out more about this bird and what happens to its young ones.

I. Picture Talk

1. This is a spiny anteater. How does it reproduce? What is its body covered with?

2. Label the diagram.

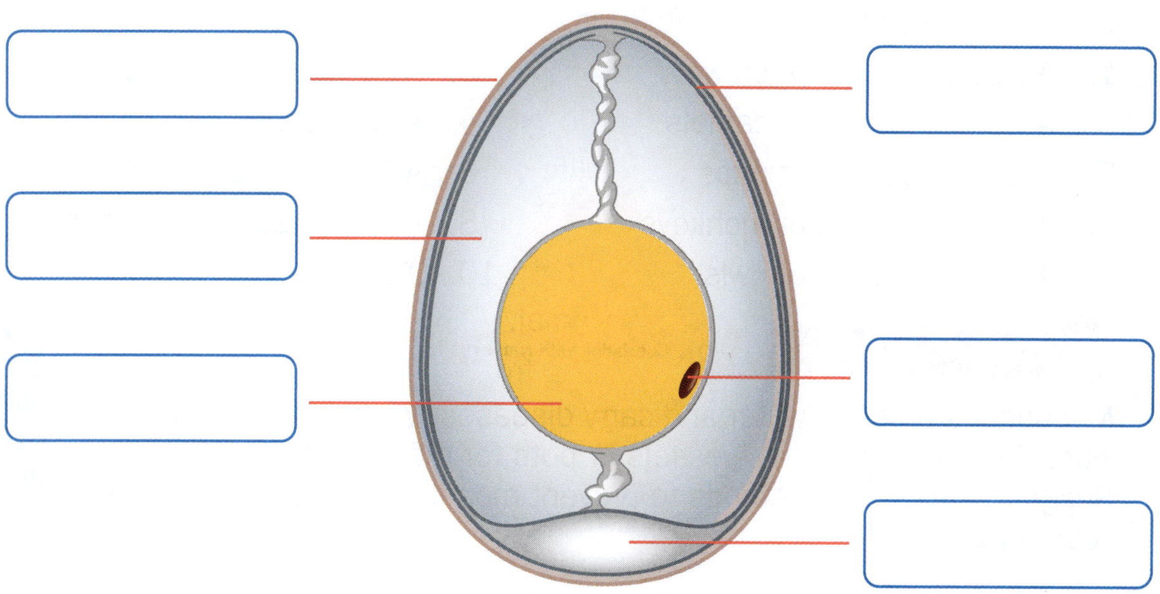

Skills Enrichment ZONE

A. 21 CS Creativity and Innovation | AI

14 LIFE BELOW WATER | 15 LIFE ON LAND

Choose one land animal and make a dangler of its life cycle. You will require three or four old greeting cards. Draw and colour the stages of the life cycle on each card. Attach the cards to each other with a piece of string. The first card will show the first stage and the last one will show the last stage. Now, hang them up on your classroom wall. Similarly, make a life cycle dangler for an animal that lives in water.

B. 21 CS Creativity and Innovation, Collaboration | AI | CC Integration with Mathematics

Make an egg carton caterpillar!

Get a 12-egg container. With the help of an elder, cut it in half length-wise. Turn it upside down. Now paint different segments of the carton in different colours and let it dry. Take five pipe cleaners and cut them into small equal pieces. Tape them to the bottom of each segment of the carton to make the legs. Make its face by sticking two paper eyes and a paper mouth in the first segment. Punch two holes on top and pass small pieces of pipe cleaners to make the antennae!

C. 21 CS Critical Thinking | CC Integration with English

Write collective nouns for the following.

1. A ______________ of crows
2. A ______________ of bees
3. A ______________ of camels
4. A ______________ of lions
5. A ______________ of pups
6. A ______________ of fish
7. A ______________ of monkeys
8. A ______________ of geese
9. A ______________ of owls
10. A ______________ of cattle

D. 21 CS Critical Thinking, Life Skills | HQ Coexisting with Nature

3 GOOD HEALTH AND WELL-BEING

Mosquitoes breed in water and carry diseases. We must not allow water to collect in drains, vessels or pots for many days at a time. Suggest a few more methods to prevent mosquitoes from breeding in your surrounding.

4 Adaptation in Animals

Prior Knowledge

In the previous classes, I have learnt that

- Animals may be wild or domestic.
- Different animals show different eating habits.
- Animals may live on land, on trees, in water and in both land and water.
- Animals living in different places have different bodily features.

Learning Objectives

In this chapter, I will learn about:

- Classification of animals
- Adaptation to the environment (habitat)
- Adaptation for protection
- Adaptation for food
- Camouflage
- Endangered animals

Let's Get Going

Look at these pictures. How are they similar and different?

____

____

____

CLASSIFICATION OF ANIMALS

There are several types of animals on Earth. They have different features that help them to survive. In this chapter, we will learn about various animals and some adaptions that they develop for survival.

Based on body structure

Animals can be classified into two groups: animals with backbones called vertebrates and animals without backbones called invertebrates. The body of an invertebrate may be soft as they have no bones but may have a hard outer covering.

Remember

The backbone is made up of a series of bones called vertebrae that are stacked together to form a column called the spinal column.

Vertebrates

Vertebrates may be classified as mammals, birds, reptiles, fish and amphibians.

Mammals: Mammals are animals that give birth to young ones of their own kind and **suckle** them. They have hair or fur as an outer covering that keeps them warm and protects them from any skin injury.

Aquatic mammals like dolphins and whales breathe through their lungs and come up to the surface to take in air.

Cow with its calf

Real World

Marsupials such as kangaroos and koalas give birth to very small new borns that crawl into their mothers' pouch to suckle and grow. They remain there till they start looking like adults.

Birds: Birds are special as they are the only animals with an outer covering of feathers. They also have wings and light hollow bones. Most birds can fly. Some birds such as penguin, ostrich and kiwi are called **flightless birds** as they cannot fly. Like mammals, birds are also warm-blooded and breathe through their lungs.

Pigeon

Your Task

What is an egg tooth in a bird?

Talk About

Why do birds need a sharp eyesight?

Fish: Fish live in water. They have scales covering their bodies. They breathe through their gills and use fins to swim. Fish are cold-blooded animals, which means their temperature changes with the change in temperature in the water.

Fish

Frog

Amphibians: Amphibians can live both on land and in water. They have moist skin. Their bodies are not covered with hair, fur, scales or feathers. They are cold-blooded animals. Most of them breathe through their lungs or skin. Frogs, salamanders and toads are amphibians.

Real World

Some salamanders live in water and breathe through their gills, while others live on land and breathe through lungs.

Reptiles: Most reptiles live on land. They have dry skin. Their bodies are covered with scales. They are cold-blooded animals. They breathe through their lungs and lay eggs. Snakes, lizards and crocodiles are reptiles. Aquatic reptiles come up to the surface to breathe through their lungs.

Crocodile

Remember

Turtle's shell is connected to its backbones. So, it cannot fall out of its shell.

Invertebrates

Insects, slugs, snails, spiders, worms and ants are all invertebrates. An insect's body has a hard outer covering called an **exoskeleton**. All insects have six legs, three body parts (head, thorax and abdomen), two eyes and two antennae (feelers). Some insects have wings.

Grasshopper

Real World

Spiders are not insects. Spiders are known as **arachnids** because they have only two body segments instead of three. They have eight legs and no wings. They have two eyes but no antennae or feelers. Other arachnids are scorpions, mites and ticks.

Spider

Knowledge Check

Fill in the blanks.

1. Animals with a backbone are called __________ (vertebrates/invertebrates).
2. Animals that can live both on land and in water are __________ (fish/amphibians).
3. Reptiles breathe through __________ (gills/lungs).
4. Mammals are __________ (warm/cold) blooded animals.

Adaptation to the environment (habitat)

We can classify animals according to the environment they live in. They can be divided into terrestrial, aquatic, arboreal, aerial and amphibians. Just like plants, animals adapt themselves to their surroundings.

Terrestrial animals

Animals that live on land are called terrestrial animals. They have features suitable for life on land. The living conditions vary from mountains, plains and deserts to polar regions.

Polar regions are extremely cold. Animals that live here, like the polar bear, Arctic foxes and walruses, have thick hair to keep them warm.

Polar bear

Penguins, seals, walruses and polar bears have a thick layer of fat under their skin called **blubber** to protect them from extreme cold.

Walrus

Food is difficult to find in winter. So, animals such as bears, frogs and snakes prefer to sleep during the winter season. This winter sleep is called **hibernation**.

Mountain goats and yaks living in the mountains also have thick coats of fur and strong hooves to walk along the mountain slopes.

Some animals such as lizards and snails sleep through the summer months to escape the heat. This long summer sleep is called **aestivation**.

Some animals that live in very cold places move to warmer places in search of food. This is called **migration**. After the winter months, they return to their homes.

Yak

Snail

Real World

Let us look at the special features of a camel that help it adapt itself to the desert environment.

- A camel's fat-filled hump provides energy during the long periods when it does not have access to food or water.
- It has two rows of long eyelashes that protect it against blowing sand and the sun.
- Its nostrils can be closed to keep out blowing sand.
- It has long strong legs that help to carry heavy loads over long distances and keep its body further away from the hot sand.

Camel

- The broad, flat and leathery pads at the bottom of its hooves prevent the camel from sinking into the sand.

Aquatic animals

Animals that live in water are called aquatic animals. Most aquatic animals have fins or paddle-like flippers that help them swim. Most aquatic animals breathe through their gills except dolphins and whales that breathe through lungs. Fish, turtles, seahorses, penguins, octopuses and crabs are aquatic animals.

Turtle

Penguin

Amphibians

Animals such as frogs, toads and salamanders that can live both on land and water are called amphibians. They have lungs that help them breathe on land and moist skin that helps them breathe in water.

Frogs and toads have strong hind (back) legs that enable them to jump and webbed feet that help them swim in water.

Frog

Remember

Frogs do not drink water as they absorb it directly through their skin.

Arboreal animals

Land animals that live mostly on trees are called arboreal animals. They have sharp claws and strong muscular limbs to climb up and down the branches of trees. Monkeys use their tails to hang on to the branches. Koalas, monkeys and squirrels are arboreal animals.

Squirrel

Aerial animals

Animals that fly and spend a lot of time in the air are called aerial animals. The shape of their body, hollow and light bones and strong wings help them fly. All birds except the flightless ones (such as kiwi, emu, penguins, ostrich) are aerial animals. Bats also belong to this family.

Real World

Bats are the only mammals that can fly. The scientific name of bats is Chiroptera ('cheir' means hand and 'pteron' means wing).

Adaptation for protection

Some animals show adaptation to protect themselves from their enemies or when in danger.

- Some herbivorous animals such as zebras, deer, rabbits and antelopes have strong legs that help them to run away from the enemy very fast.

Zebra

- Elephants and rhinoceros have thick skins that protect them from heat.

Elephant

- Crabs, turtles, tortoises and clams have hard shells to protect their soft bodies.

Tortoise

- Cockroaches and beetles have a hard outer body for protection.

Beetle

- A porcupine has sharp quills to protect itself.

Porcupine

- A rhinoceros has a horn that it uses as a weapon.

Rhinoceros

- Some animals such as hyenas, elephants and fish stay in groups for safety.

Hyenas

- Animals such as cuttlefish and squids release an inky fluid when attacked.

Cuttlefish

- Skunks release a strong bad smell to keep their enemies away.

Skunk

- Wasps and scorpions sting their enemies to protect themselves.

Wasp

Adaptation for food

Animals can also be classified according to their food habits into herbivores, carnivores, omnivores, scavengers and parasites.

- **Herbivores**

  Herbivores are the animals that eat only plants.They have sharp front teeth for biting and cutting and strong hind teeth for grinding their food.

Deer

- **Carnivores**

  Carnivores are the animals that eat flesh.They are also called **predators** and the animals that they hunt, kill and eat are called **prey**. They have long, sharp, curved and pointed teeth to tear flesh and broad hind teeth to chew flesh and bones.

Tiger

- **Omnivores**

  Omnivores are animals that eat both plants and animals.

Crow

- **Scavengers**

  Scavengers are animals that feed on dead animals. By doing this, they clean the Earth of organic garbage.

Vulture

- **Parasites**

  Parasites are animals that live in or on another living thing and get their food from them. Lice and fleas live on a host body and suck its blood for food.

Flea

Louse

CAMOUFLAGE

The colour and shape of some animals help them merge with the surrounding environment. This is called camouflage. This helps the animals to protect themselves as they remain unnoticed by their enemies.

- The white fur of the polar bear and Arctic fox merges with the snow.
- Tigers have stripes and lions have a colour that helps them to merge with the forest or grassland.

Arctic fox

Tiger

- A stick insect that looks like a twig or a grasshopper's green colour merges with the leaves', making it difficult for its enemies to spot them.

Grasshopper

ENDANGERED ANIMALS

Animals such as dodo are no longer found on Earth. They are called extinct animals. Dinosaurs that lived millions of years ago are also extinct animals.

Human beings are destroying the homes of animals by cutting down trees, destroying forests, polluting rivers and seas and even killing animals for skin, flesh and bones.

Your Task

What is WWF? Why does it use the picture of a panda as its emblem? Find out what it means.

Tigers, cheetahs, giant pandas and rhinoceros are becoming fewer in number. These animals are in the danger of disappearing from the Earth. Such animals are called endangered animals.

Concept Map

Adaptation According to Environment

- **Terrestrial** (Land) Examples: Horse, rhinoceros, deer
- **Aquatic** (Water) Examples: Fish, dolphin, crab
- **Amphibian** (Water and land) Examples: Toad, frog, salamander
- **Arboreal** (Trees) Examples: Monkey, squirrel, koala
- **Aerial** (Air) Examples: Birds, bat

Adaptation According to Food Habit

- **Carnivores** (Eat only animals) Examples: Lion, tiger
- **Herbivores** (Plant-eating) Examples: Giraffe, deer
- **Omnivores** (Eat both plants and animals) Examples: Bear, crow
- **Scavengers** (Feed on dead animals) Examples: Hyena, vulture
- **Parasites** (Live on or inside another animal) Examples: Louse, hookworm

Summary

a. In this chapter, I have learnt that

- Vertebrates are animals with backbones and invertebrates are animals without backbones.
- Based on their habitats, animals can be classified into terrestrial, aquatic, amphibians, arboreal and aerial.
- Based on their food habits, animals can be classified as herbivores, carnivores, omnivores, scavengers and parasites.
- Camouflage is a way by which animals merge with their surroundings to protect themselves.
- Endangered animals are those which are in the danger of disappearing from the Earth.

b. I can do the following:

- Identify animals with or without backbones
- Explain how animals adapt to the surroundings they live in or based on their feeding habits
- List the different ways animals protect themselves in times of danger

Practice ZONE

A. Choose the correct option.

1. __________ is a reptile.

   a. Lizard b. Salamander c. Kiwi

2. __________ is the process of moving from cold to warm places in search of food.

   a. Hibernation b. Migration c. Aestivation

3. __________ uses its horn as a weapon.

   a. Unicorn b. Hippopotamus c. Rhinoceros

4. __________ is difficult to spot on a tree.

   a. Stick insect b. Beetle c. Butterfly

B. Write T for true or F for false.

1. Fish are cold-blooded animals.
2. Insects have a hard-inner covering called exoskeleton.
3. A porcupine has sharp quills to protect itself.
4. A skunk releases an inky fluid when attacked.

C. Fill in the blanks using the words given in the box.

eight	scales	hard shell	elephants

1. Fish have __________ covering their bodies.
2. Spiders have __________ legs.
3. __________ have thick skins that protect them from heat.
4. A tortoise has a __________ __________ to protect its soft body.

D. Give two examples for each of these.

1. Flightless birds
2. Amphibians
3. Terrestrial animals in polar regions
4. Arboreal animals

E. Give reasons for each of these.

1. An ostrich is the fastest running bird, but it cannot fly.
2. Frogs and ducks have webbed feet.

F. Answer these questions in brief.

1. How do aquatic mammals breathe?
2. Describe the parts of an insect's body.
3. What is blubber?
4. What are aerial animals?

G. Answer these questions in detail.

1. Describe the structure of a bird.
2. Describe the characteristics of the four classes of animals based on their food habits.
3. Draw a bird and label its body parts.

H. Out of the box!

How do humans adapt to their surroundings? What part of our body helps us in adapting?

I. Picture Talk

1. Why do you think the polar bear is looking sad?

2. How do the following animals protect themselves?

a.  ________________

____

b.  ________________

____

Skills Enrichment ZONE

A. 21 CS Creativity and Innovation, Collaboration | AI | CC Integration with Mathematics | HQ Happiness My Goal

Make finger puppets!

Material required:

- Old cards
- Glue
- Colour pencils

Method:

- With the help of an elder, cut a card into two halves.
- Cut out shape of an animal from one half of the card.
- Make eyes, nose and mouth of the animal.
- Roll the other half of the card into a cylinder that fits your finger.
- Now, paste the animal face on the top end of the cylinder. Your finger puppet is ready! Try out making more puppets for your fingers.

B. 21 CS Critical Thinking, Communication | HQ How Similar are We | CC Integration with English

15 LIFE ON LAND

Do you think it is right to put animals in cages and in zoos? Discuss with your classmates and write a few lines about this in your diary.

C. 21 CS Critical Thinking, Life Skills | IF | CC Integration with English | HQ Coexisting with Nature

13 CLIMATE ACTION

Choose one animal found in India that is endangered. Write a story keeping an animal as the main character. In your story, tell why that animal is endangered and how it can be saved.

Worksheet 2

STEAM CHALLENGE

Sirat is Siraj's younger sister. She likes aquarium very much. However, she does not want to keep an aquarium with living fish. She thinks it is not right. Siraj wants to make an aquatic diorama (a three-dimensional model) for his sister.

Help Siraj create a beautiful aquatic diorama.

What is the challenge?

What supplies do you need?

1

2

What worked or did not work for you?

How can you improve it?

5 Food and Health

Prior Knowledge

In the previous classes, I have learnt that

- Food provides us energy to do work.
- Food is obtained mainly from plants and animals.
- We should eat healthy food to stay healthy.

Learning Objectives

In this chapter, I will learn about:

- Nutrients
- Food groups
- Balanced diet
- Food preservation
- Rest and exercise

Let's Get Going

Classify these food items into plant or animal products.

Papaya	Bread	Apple	Egg
Chapati	Noodles	Dal	Fish
Meat	Banana	Milk	Butter
Cauliflower	Rice	Spinach	Curd

Plant products	Animal products

NUTRIENTS

All living things need food to grow, keep healthy and get energy for various activities. The substances present in our food that help our body to grow and stay healthy are called nutrients.

Food groups

Nutrients present in the food can be divided into five main groups according to the function they perform in the body. They are carbohydrates, fats, proteins, vitamins and minerals. Food also contains water and roughage.

Carbohydrates

Carbohydrates are called **energy-giving foods**. They are the main source of energy for our bodies. Carbohydrates are of two types, starch and sugar. Wheat, bread, potatoes and rice contain starch. Chocolates, cakes, sweets and fruits such as bananas and cheekoo contain sugar. People who do a lot of physical work such as sportsmen, labourers and even children need to have a lot of carbohydrates.

Bread

Potato

Banana

Rice

Fats

Fats also provide us energy. In fact, they give us more energy than carbohydrates do. Oil, nuts, butter, cheese, ghee, fried food and junk food are some food items rich in fats.

Fats also keep our bodies warm. When we consume more fat than what is needed by our body, it is stored in the body for future use. We should not consume excess fat as it is not good for our health.

Oil

Nuts

Butter

Cheese

Proteins

Proteins are **body-building** and **body-repairing** nutrients. They help in the growth and development of our body. Fish, meat, eggs, milk, beans, cheese, pulses (or daal) and tofu are rich in proteins.

It is important for children to have protein-rich food as it helps them to grow. When we get hurt and damage our body, proteins help in repairing the body by making new cells.

Eggs

Fish

Pulses

Meat

Vitamins and minerals

Vitamins and minerals protect our body from diseases and keep us healthy. Thus, they are known as **protective food**. Fresh fruits, milk, fresh vegetables, fish, eggs and meat are rich in vitamins and minerals. A little portion of vitamins and minerals should be taken in every meal.

Some of the important minerals are iron, calcium, sodium and potassium. Iron is required for making blood in our body and can be found in leafy vegetables (spinach) and fruits (bananas). Calcium makes our bones and teeth strong and is found in milk and milk products. Table salt contains sodium. Bananas contain potassium.

Fresh fruits and vegetables

Milk

Water

Seventy per cent of a human body is made up of water. During the day, as we do different activities, our body loses water. It is important to drink lots of water every day as the loss of it can cause dehydration (when you lose more water than what you take in). Water helps digest food and move out wastes from our body. Our food, specially some juicy fruits and vegetables, also contains water.

Roughage

Roughage is the fibre obtained from the plant food we eat. It is a part of the food that cannot be digested but helps in getting rid of the undigested food. We get roughage from leafy vegetables, fresh fruits and cereals.

Your Task

Take an orange and peel it. Put an orange wedge into your mouth and chew till you are left with a fibre-like thing in your mouth. That is roughage!

Knowledge Check

Match the following.

1. Carbohydrates	a. Butter
2. Fats	b. Pulses
3. Proteins	c. Fruits
4. Vitamins	d. Potato

BALANCED DIET

To be healthy, our diet must contain each nutrient in the right **proportion**. Such a diet is called a balanced diet. It helps our mind and body to grow well and gives us ample energy. The rules of a balanced diet are:

- Drink plenty of water.
- Eat lots of fruits and vegetables.
- Eat carbohydrates such as rice and chapati.
- Avoid taking too much salt or salty food.
- Eat fish, meat, eggs or pulses, tofu, etc.
- Cut down on fat and sweets.
- Get active and exercise daily.

Balanced diet

My Dictionary

proportion: amount

Knowledge Check

Are you eating healthy?

Tick 'Yes' or 'No' to answer these questions.

Question	Yes	No
Do you have a fruit every day?		
Do you avoid eating chips every day?		
Do you have milk or milk products two times a day?		
Do you have a glass of juice every day?		
Do you chew your food well while eating?		

How many times did you tick "Yes"?

5: You have a healthy way of living.

4: You eat well.

3: Try to eat healthier food.

2: You need to be careful with your diet.

1: You need to check your food habit.

0: You need to visit a doctor.

FOOD PRESERVATION

When food is not stored properly, it gets spoilt. Germs or moulds grow on it. You must have seen green fungus growing on slices of bread when it turns stale. Thus, it is important to preserve food if we want to store it for a longer time. The process of preventing food from getting spoilt is called food preservation.

The different methods of preserving food are:

Refrigerating: Storing food at a low temperature helps keep away germs. Thus, fruits, vegetables and cooked food are kept inside a refrigerator to prevent them from getting spoilt.

Refrigerating

Cooking: Some food items can be eaten raw but most of them have to be cooked. Cooking not only kills germs but also makes food softer, tastier and easy to digest. Some of the methods of cooking are boiling, roasting, frying and baking.

Canning: Canning is a method in which food items like jams and juices are first heated to a high temperature, then cooled and put into airtight containers.

Drying: In this method, the food items are dried completely. For example, some food items like mint, red chillies and raisins are preserved after water has been removed from them. This helps in preventing the growth of germs.

Cooking

Canning

Drying

Adding preservatives: Sometimes certain chemicals are added to food to prevent it from getting spoilt. These chemicals are called **preservatives**. Some common preservatives are salt, oil, vinegar and sugar.

- **Pickling:** Adding salt and oil to preserve pickles
- **Jellying:** Adding sugar syrup to make jams and jellies

Pickling

Your Task

CC Integration with Mathematics

Make a Glow Salad!

Ingredients:

1 cup boiled peas, $\frac{1}{2}$ cup boiled corn, $\frac{1}{2}$ cup finely chopped tomato, $\frac{1}{2}$ cup finely chopped capsicum, $\frac{1}{2}$ cup finely chopped onions, $\frac{1}{2}$ cup finely chopped cucumber

Dressing:

Mix 1 tablespoon white oil, $1\frac{1}{2}$ tablespoon lemon juice, 2 tablespoon tomato sauce, 1 tablespoon garlic chilli sauce, 1 level teaspoon sugar, $\frac{1}{4}$ teaspoon black pepper, $\frac{1}{2}$ teaspoon salt. Your dressing is ready for use.

Method:

Mix the above ingredients in a bowl. Add $\frac{1}{2}$ teaspoon red chilli powder and $\frac{1}{2}$ teaspoon roasted jeera or cumin powder. Then add the dressing. Toss the salad and refrigerate.

REST AND EXERCISE

Have you ever heard of a couch potato? A **couch potato** is a person who does little or no exercise and watches a lot of television.

A couch potato

Along with a balanced diet, our body needs rest and exercise. Regular exercise is important as it keeps us healthy and fit. It makes our bones and muscles strong, and our body fit and full of energy. Exercise also makes our muscles and heart strong. Practising yoga is also good as it makes our body and mind feel relaxed. We must also sleep seven to eight hours every day to stay healthy.

A girl doing yoga

A boy sleeping

Your Task

CC Integration with Mathematics

Let's do some fun exercises.

- Hop 10 times standing in one place.
- Circle your arms five times.
- Jog standing in one place for 5 minutes.
- Touch your toes and then stand up. Do this ten times.

Concept Map

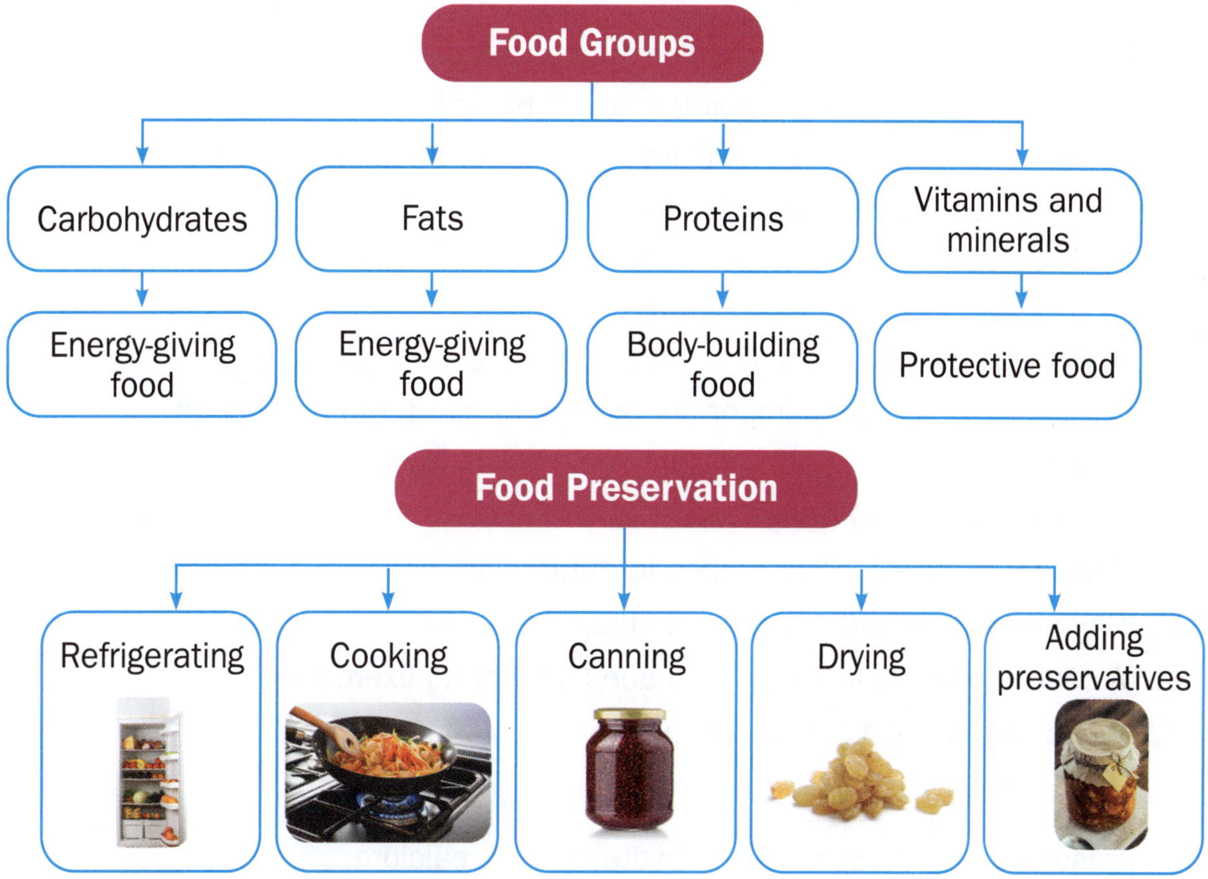

Summary

a. In this chapter, I have learnt that

- Nutrients are substances found in our food that help us to grow and stay healthy.
- The five food groups are carbohydrates, fats, proteins, vitamins and minerals.
- 70% of our body is made of water.
- Roughage helps us get rid of undigested food.
- A balanced diet contains each nutrient in the right amount.
- The different methods of food preservation are cooking, freezing, canning, drying and adding preservatives like pickling and jellying.

b. I can do the following:

- Name the foods that belong to different food groups
- Understand the importance of drinking enough water
- Explain the importance of a balanced diet, rest and exercise
- Choose my food responsibly

Practice ZONE

A. Choose the correct option.

1. ______________ is a mineral found in table salt.
   a. Iron b. Calcium c. Sodium
2. ______________ is a preservative.
   a. Vinegar b. Chilli sauce c. Soya sauce
3. ______________ give us roughage.
   a. Chocolates b. Fresh fruits c. Milk products
4. ______________ is an important mineral for our teeth and bones.
   a. Iron b. Calcium c. Sodium

B. Write T for true or F for false.

1. Extra fat is stored in our bodies for future use.
2. Children should avoid proteins in their diet.
3. A couch potato is a person who does little or no exercise.
4. We should sleep 12 hours every day.

C. Fill in the blanks.

preserved	fungus	dehydration	calcium

1. Not having enough water in the body can lead to ______________.
2. ______________ makes our bones and teeth strong.
3. When bread becomes stale, ______________ grows on it.
4. Low temperature inside a freezer keeps the food ______________.

D. Give two examples for each of these.

1. Food rich in carbohydrates
2. Food rich in proteins
3. Methods of preserving food

E. Give reasons for these.

1. We should include fats in our diet.
2. We should not eat pizzas and burgers only.
3. We should drink a lot of water in summer.

F. Answer these questions in brief.

1. What are nutrients? Name the five main groups of nutrients.
2. Who needs a carbohydrate-rich diet?

3. What is roughage? How can we include roughage in our diet?
4. What is canning?

G. Answer these questions in detail.

1. Write a note on why minerals and vitamins are important elements in our diet.
2. Write down the rules of a balanced diet.

H. Out of the box!

A baby has only mother's milk for the first few months of its life. Yet it grows very fast. How does it get all the nutrients?

I. Picture Talk

Look at the given picture and answer the questions that follow.

1. What does this diagram show?
2. What kind of food do you need the least and the most? Why?

Skills Enrichment ZONE

A. 21 CS Communication, Life Skills | HQ Cooperation and Collaborative Living | CC Integration with Mathematics

Conduct a survey to collect data on "Favourite Breakfast".

Ask your friends about their favourite breakfast from the given list and mention the number of students against each food item.

	Food items	Number of students who like them
1	Toast	
2	Sandwich	
3	Cornflakes	
4	Porridge	
5	Idli	
6	Dosa	
7	Pizza	
8	Others	

Which is the most favourite breakfast item? ____________________

B. 21 CS Critical Thinking, Life Skills | CC Integration with Mathematics | HQ Knowing My Needs

3 GOOD HEALTH AND WELL-BEING

Make a list of all the food items that you had for breakfast, lunch and dinner yesterday.

Breakfast: ______________________________

Lunch: ______________________________

Dinner: ______________________________

Classify them into different food groups.

Carbohydrates	Fats	Proteins	Vitamins	Minerals

Answer these questions based on your classification.

- Did you have food from all the food groups? (Yes/No)
- Was your diet balanced? (Yes/No)
- If not, which food group was missing in your diet?
- What could you have eaten to make your diet balanced?
- How many glasses of water did you drink yesterday?

C. 21 CS Creativity and Innovation | AI | HQ Harmony in Relationships

Fun with Fingers!

Next time, when you have some guests over for dinner, try decorating the table for them with this bunny idea. Click a picture of the bunny and paste in your art book. Did you enjoy doing this activity?

6 Teeth and Microbes

Prior Knowledge

In the previous classes, I have learnt that

- We have 32 teeth.
- Teeth help us bite, chew and grind the food.
- We should take care of our teeth.

Learning Objectives

In this chapter, I will learn about:

- Structure of a tooth
- Types of teeth
- Care of teeth
- Microbes

Let's Get Going

Write three things that we can do with our teeth in the boxes.

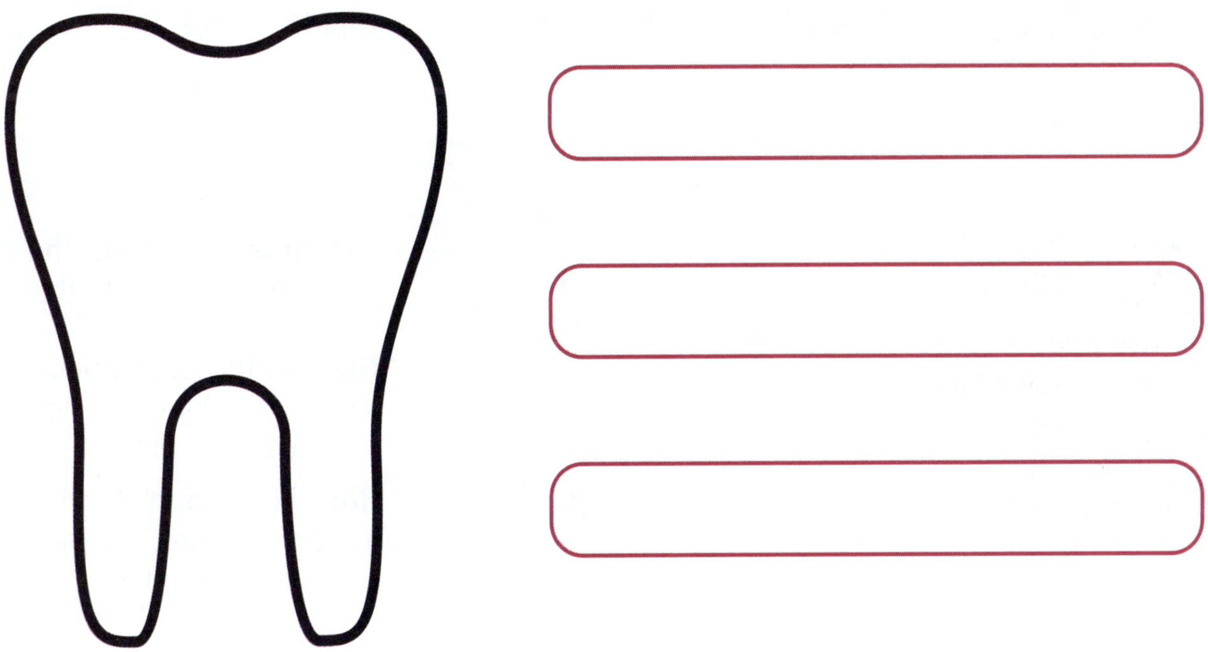

TEETH

We need teeth not only to bite and chew but also to talk, smile and whisper.

Babies are born without any teeth. By the time they are six months old, they get their first tooth and by the age of three, they have up to twenty teeth. This set of teeth is called the **milk teeth** or **temporary teeth**. By five or six years of age, the milk teeth start falling and are replaced by a set of **permanent teeth**. An adult has 32 permanent teeth.

Toothless baby

Structure of a tooth

A tooth has three layers: enamel, dentine and pulp.

A tooth is made up of three parts: crown, neck and root.

Talk About

- Who is an orthodontist?
- What are deciduous teeth?

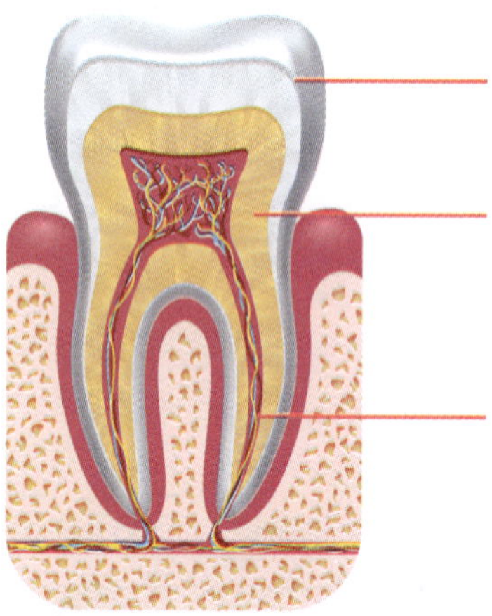

Layers of a tooth

The outermost layer is the **enamel**. It is the hardest part of the body. It protects the tooth from decay.

The next layer is the **dentine**. It lies just below the enamel and is not as hard as the enamel. The dentine forms the bulk of the tooth and has a yellowish colour.

The **pulp** is found inside the dentine. Pulp is the soft part of the tooth and has nerves and blood vessels. The tooth receives its nourishment from the pulp.

Remember

No two people have the same set of teeth. Every person's teeth are unique just like their fingerprints.

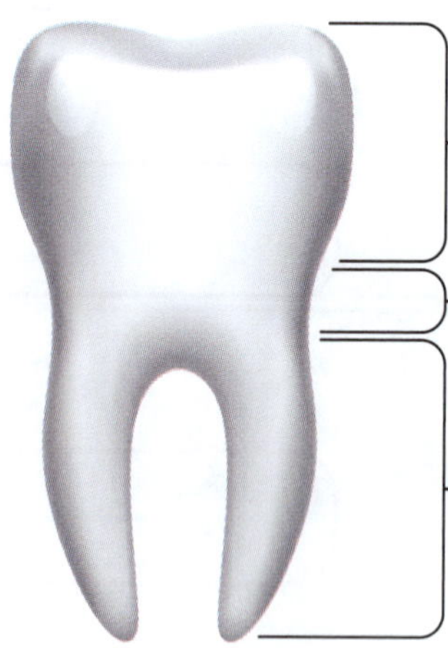

Parts of a tooth

Crown is the part of the tooth that we see outside the gum.

Neck is the part found below the crown where the tooth touches the gum.

Root is the part that is found inside the gum. It helps the tooth to be in place.

Types of teeth

> **Your Task**
>
> Why do some children wear braces on their teeth?

An adult has four types of teeth. They are incisors, canines, premolars and molars.

- **Incisors** help us to bite and cut the food. There are eight incisors, four in each jaw.
- **Canines** are the sharp, pointed teeth found next to the incisors. They help in tearing the food. There are four canines, two on each jaw.
- Next to the canines are the **premolars**. They are flat, broad teeth that help in chewing, crushing and grinding. There are eight premolars, four on each jaw.
- Behind the premolars are the **molars**. They are broader than the premolars and help in chewing, grinding and crushing. There are twelve molars in all.

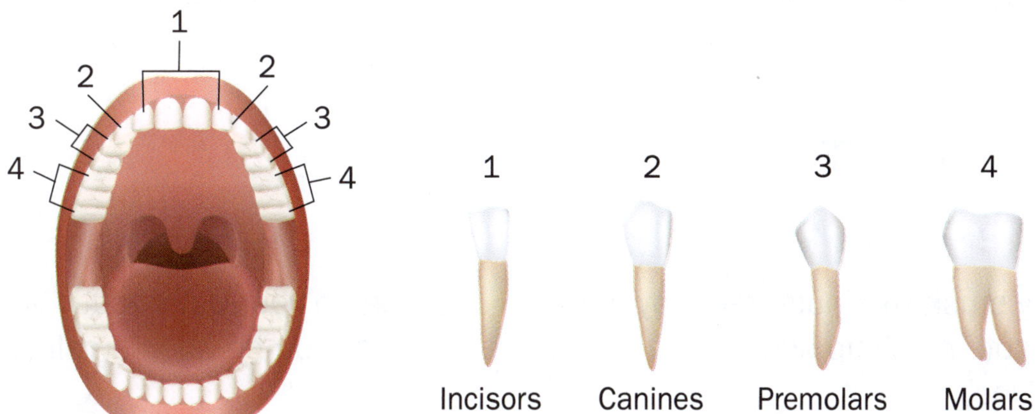

Arrangement of teeth in humans

CARE OF TEETH

Teeth play an important role in our digestion process. Hence, it is important that we take care of them.

> **Science in Action**
>
> We use dental floss to remove the food particles stuck between our teeth. This is called flossing.

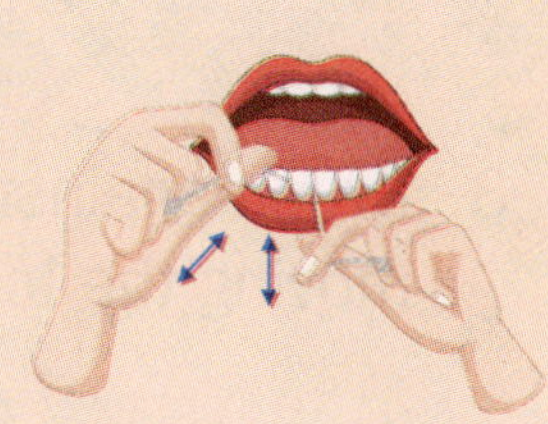

When we eat, some of the food particles get stuck in between our teeth. If not removed, bacteria and germs feed on these food particles and damage our teeth. This leads to the formation of **cavities** or holes in the enamel. The cavity grows bigger and bigger till it reaches the nerves and that is when we get a toothache.

Over a period, our teeth get covered by a sticky, yellow substance called **plaque**. It is important that we keep our teeth clean to avoid gum diseases and formation of plaque.

Here are some of the ways in which you can keep your teeth clean and healthy.

- Brush your teeth twice every day, in the morning and before going to bed.
- Brush all your teeth, not just the front ones. Be sure to brush along the sides and at the back.
- Change your toothbrush every three months.
- Rinse your mouth after eating anything, especially after having sweets or desserts.
- Clean your tongue after you brush your teeth.
- Take calcium-rich food such as milk to make your teeth strong.
- Visit a dentist regularly for a check-up.

Talk About

What do you think will happen if you do not brush your teeth for a few days?

Following steps show the right way to brush your teeth:

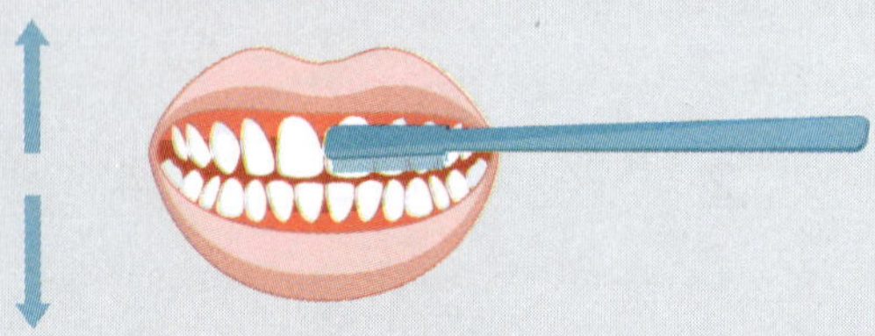

1. Softly brush your outer teeth by moving the tooth brush up and down all along the gum line.

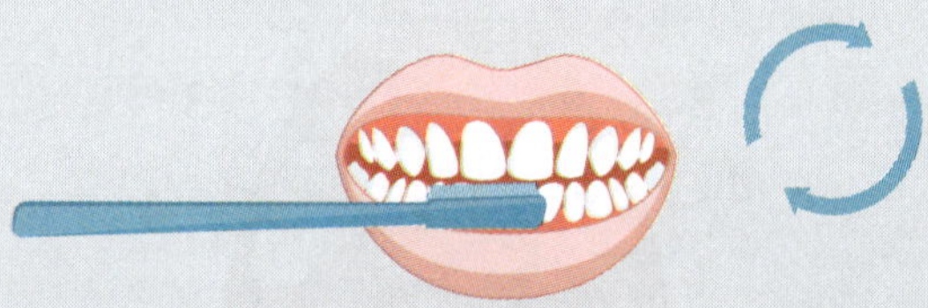

2. Brush your outer teeth by moving the toothbrush in small circles.

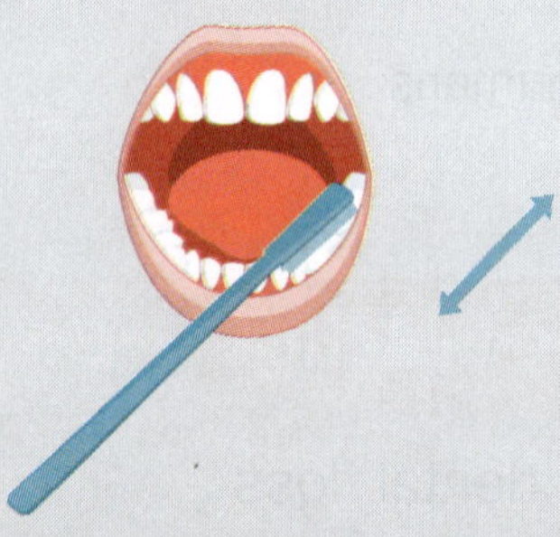

3. Brush against the top of each tooth by moving the toothbrush back and forth.

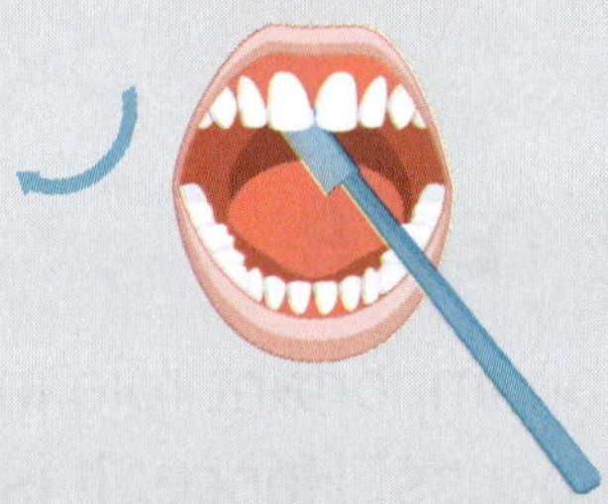

4. Softly brush your teeth on the inside by moving the toothbrush in small circles all along the gum line.

Knowledge Check

Fill in the blanks.

1. The three parts of a tooth are ____________, ____________ and ____________.
2. Teeth used for biting are called ____________.
3. Teeth used for tearing are called ____________.
4. Teeth used for grinding are called ____________ and ____________.

MICROBES

There are many tiny little organisms around us that are so small that it is impossible to see them with the naked eye. These are called microbes. You need a **microscope** to see them. There are four main types of microbes: bacteria, virus, fungi and protozoa.

My Dictionary

microscope: an instrument that makes small things appear big

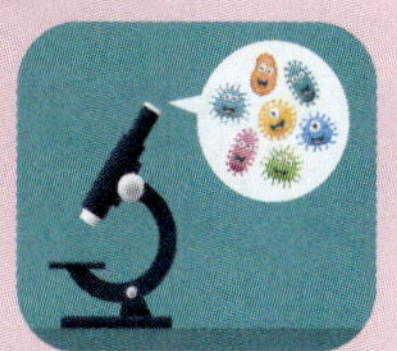

Bacteria

Bacteria can be found almost everywhere. They are very small and made of only one cell. Some bacteria are harmful and cause diseases such as tuberculosis, pneumonia and typhoid. Some bacteria are useful, for example, bacteria that turn milk into curd; bacteria in our stomach that help digest food; and bacteria that help dead plants and animals to rot.

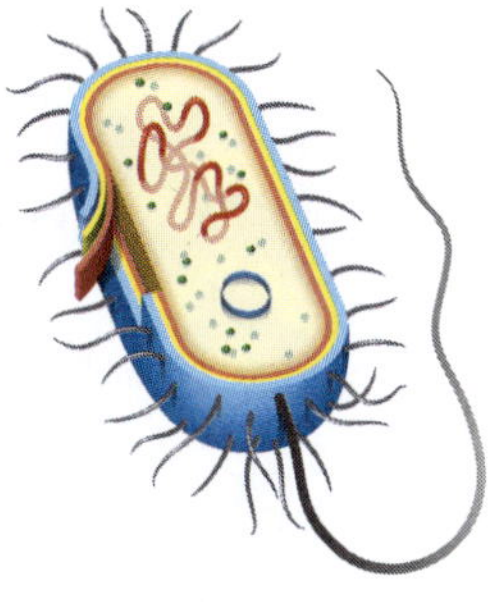

A bacterium

Viruses

Viruses are the smallest living things. They are generally harmful as they cause diseases such as common cold and chicken pox. A new virus was found in late 2019. This virus causes a deadly disease called coronavirus disease or COVID-19.

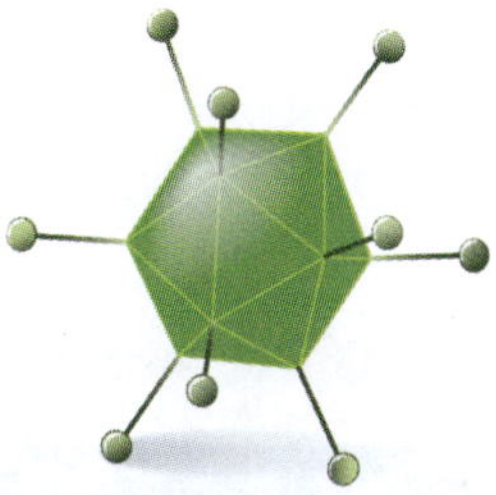

A virus

Fungi

Have you seen a mushroom? They are neither animals nor plants. They belong to a group of living things called fungi. Fungi feed on dead plants and animals around them. Some fungi are useful and used to make medicines and bread (such as yeast). Some fungi are harmful and cause diseases such as ringworms.

Fungi

Protozoa

Protozoa are also tiny organisms, though a little bigger than bacteria. They cause diseases such as malaria and dysentery.

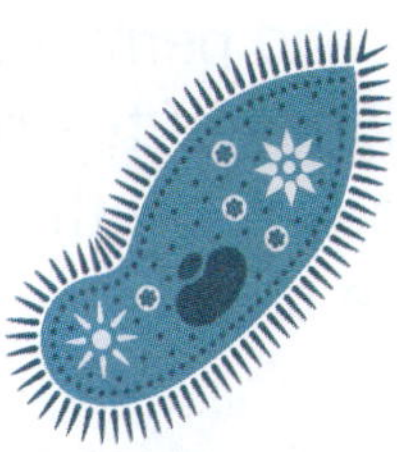

A protozoan

Your Task

Who was Edward Jenner? What did he discover?

Concept Map

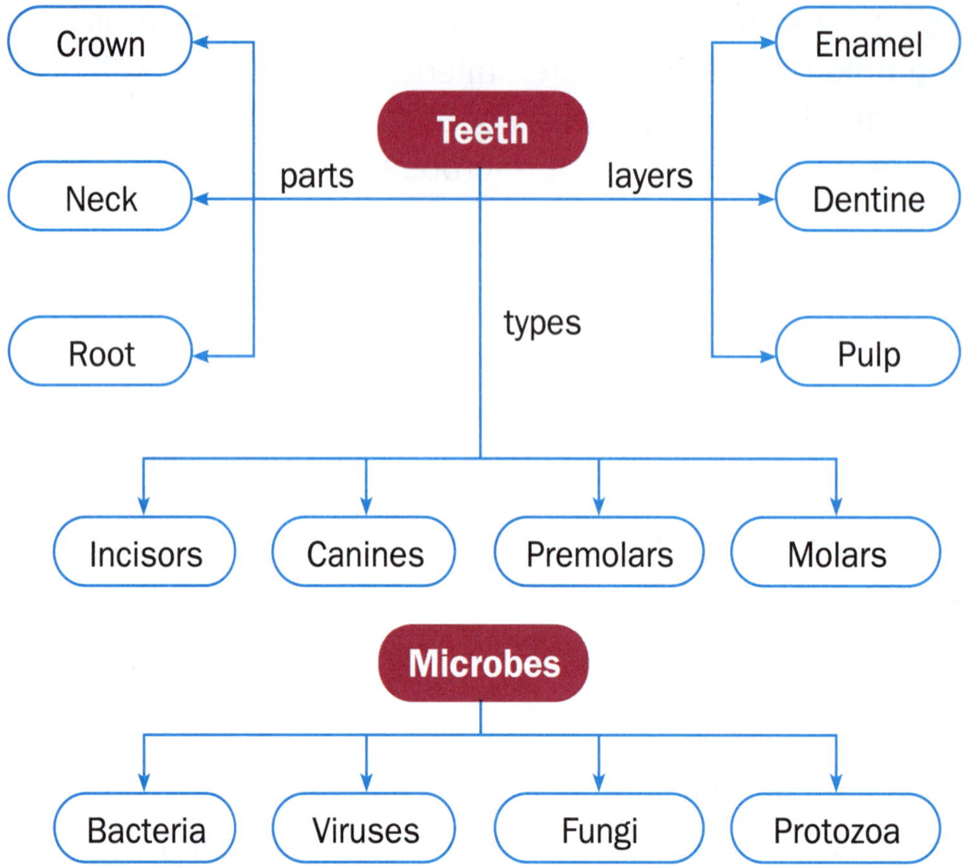

Summary

a. In this chapter, I have learnt that

- A small child has 20 temporary teeth while an adult has 32 permanent teeth.
- A tooth has three layers: enamel, dentine and pulp.
- The three parts of a tooth are crown, neck and root.
- An adult has four types of teeth: incisors, canines, premolars and molars.
- We must brush our teeth properly to keep them clean and healthy.
- The four types of microbes are bacteria, virus, fungi and protozoa.
- While some microbes make us sick, some are useful to us.

b. I can do the following:

- Understand what temporary and permanent teeth are
- Identify and name the four kinds of teeth
- State the function of the kinds of teeth
- Draw and label structure of a tooth
- List the different microbes
- Name the disease-causing and useful microbes

Practice ZONE

A. Choose the correct option.

1. ____________ is the hardest part of our body.
   a. Enamel　　b. Dentine　　c. Pulp
2. There are ____________ premolars.
   a. six　　b. eight　　c. ten
3. ____________ is caused by fungi.
   a. Malaria　　b. Cholera　　c. Ringworm
4. There are ____________ permanent teeth.
   a. 31　　b. 32　　c. 33

B. Write T for true or F for false.

1. Canines are flat, broad teeth.
2. The dentine is the layer just below the enamel.
3. Children have milk teeth.
4. Fungi are a group of plants.

C. Fill in the blanks using the words given in the box.

twice	microscope	cavities	plaque

1. We should brush our teeth ____________ a day.
2. We get toothaches because of ____________ in the tooth.
3. Sticky yellow substance formed on teeth is called ____________.
4. We need a ____________ to see microbes.

D. Give two examples for each of these.

1. Diseases caused by bacteria
2. Diseases caused by virus
3. Diseases caused by protozoa

E. Give reasons for each of these.

1. Baby teeth are also called deciduous teeth.
2. We give soft food to old people or infants.
3. We should brush our teeth before going to sleep.

F. Answer these questions in brief.

1. Why do we need teeth?
2. Write the names of the different parts of a tooth.
3. Why should we take care of our teeth?

4. How are cavities formed in our teeth?
5. How are some bacteria beneficial for us?

G. Answer these questions in detail.

1. Describe the four types of teeth and state their functions.
2. Draw a tooth and label its layers. Describe each layer.

H. Out of the box!

Which teeth are called the wisdom teeth? Why are they called so?

I. Picture Talk

1. Look at the pictures. What has gone wrong with them?

2. Identify the different kinds of teeth and write their functions.

	Name	Function

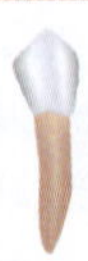		

Skills Enrichment ZONE

A. 21 CS Communication, Life Skills | CC Integration with English

3 GOOD HEALTH AND WELL-BEING

When you were young, you would have been given various vaccines from time-to-time. Ask your mother about the vaccinations and injections given to you as a baby. What diseases do they protect you from?

B. 21 CS Communication, Life Skills | CC Integration with English | HQ Cooperation and Collaborative Living

Look at the pictures of four teeth given below. What kind of conversation would they be having? Write a short story based on the conversation among the four teeth.

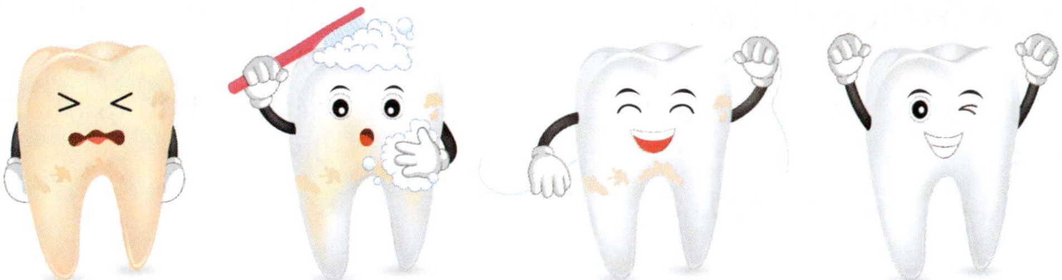

C. 21 CS Critical Thinking, Life skills | HQ Knowing My Needs

6 CLEAN WATER AND SANITATION

Our parents always ask us to wash our hands before eating and after using the toilet. Why do you think they do so? What would happen if we eat with dirty hands?

7 Digestive System

Prior Knowledge

In the previous classes, I have learnt that

- We have different organs in our body.
- The food that we eat needs to be digested.
- We should eat healthy food.

Learning Objectives

In this chapter, I will learn about:

- Organs of the digestive system
- Healthy habits related to digestion

Let's Get Going

Fill up the plate with your favourite food items.

1. ____________

2. ____________

3. ____________

4. ____________

Take a bite of a slice of bread. Chew it. How does it taste? Talk about the change in taste as you keep on chewing it.

ORGANS OF THE DIGESTIVE SYSTEM

We eat food to stay alive. The food provides us energy. The food we eat can be useful to us only when it is broken down into smaller substances that can be easily absorbed by our body. This process is called **digestion**.

Digestion takes place in the digestive system, which is a long continuous tube that starts at the mouth and ends at the anus. The organs that help in the digestion of food form the digestive system.

Talk About

Why do we need to chew our food?

Let us trace the journey of food inside the body.

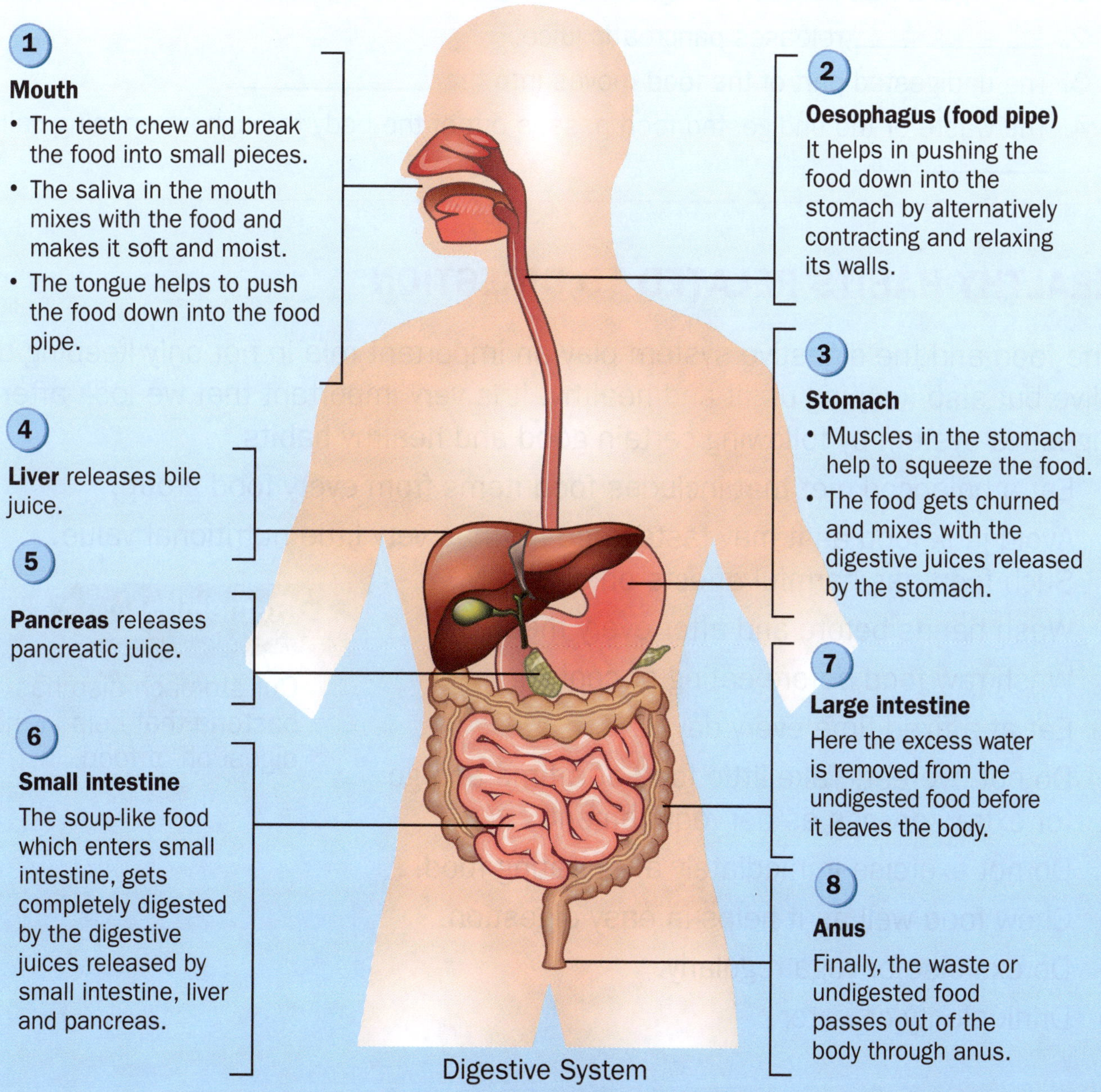

Digestive System

It takes at least four hours to digest the food we eat.

Real World

- When we see or smell our favourite food, our mouth starts watering. This is because the saliva, secreted by salivary glands, starts forming in our mouth even before we start eating.
- Our small intestine is 22 feet long. It is called the small intestine because it is small in width.

Knowledge Check

Fill in the blanks.

1. The organs that help in the digestion of food form the ______________.
2. ______________ releases pancreatic juice.
3. The undigested part of the food moves into the ______________.
4. The waste or the undigested food passes out of the body through an opening called ______________.

HEALTHY HABITS RELATED TO DIGESTION

The food and the digestive system play an important role in not only keeping us alive but also keeping us fit and healthy. It is very important that we look after our digestive system by following certain good and healthy habits.

- Eat a balanced diet that includes food items from every food group.
- Avoid junk food as it may taste good but has very little nutritional value. Such food has harmful effects on our body.
- Wash hands before and after every meal.
- Wash raw food before eating or cooking.
- Eat at a fixed time every day.
- Do not overeat. Take little food at a time and go for extra servings as per requirement.
- Do not exercise immediately after eating food.
- Chew food well as it helps in easy digestion.
- Do exercise or yoga regularly.
- Drink plenty of water

Remember

Our stomach also has bacteria that help in the digestion of food.

Concept Map

Journey of Food During Digestion

- **Mouth**
  - Teeth break the food into small pieces.
  - Saliva mixes with food and makes it soft and moist.
  - Tongue helps to swallow the chewed food.
- **Food pipe** → It pushes the food down into the stomach.
- **Stomach** → Muscles churn and mix the food with digestive juices.
- **Small intestine** → Complete digestion of food occurs with the help of digestive juices produced by small intestine, liver and pancreas.
- **Large intestine** → Excess water is removed from the undigested food.
- **Anus** → It passes the undigested food out of the body.

Summary

a. In this chapter, I have learnt that

- The breaking down of food into smaller substances that can be easily absorbed by the body is called digestion.
- The organs of the digestive system are mouth, food pipe, stomach, liver, pancreas, small intestine, large intestine and anus.
- We must avoid unhealthy food and eat a balanced diet.

b. I can do the following:

- Name the organs of the digestive system
- Describe the journey of food from the mouth till the undigested food is released through the anus
- List and follow healthy eating habits

Practice ZONE

A. Choose the correct option.

1. When we swallow, the food passes into the ________________.

   a. food pipe b. liver c. stomach

2. ________________ makes the food soft and moist inside the mouth.

   a. Tongue b. Saliva c. Teeth

3. Complete digestion of food takes place in the ________________.

   a. stomach b. small intestine c. large intestine

4. Water is removed from the food in the ________________.

   a. stomach b. small intestine c. large intestine

B. Write T for true or F for false.

1. The stomach is just a bag for holding our food.
2. It takes at least four hours to digest food.
3. It is okay to eat unwashed raw fruits.
4. We should chew our food well.

C. Fill in the blanks.

stomach anus bile juice junk

1. The food from the food pipe enters the ________________.
2. ________________ is released by the liver.
3. The undigested food passes out of our body through the ________________.
4. We should avoid eating ________________ food.

D. Give reasons for each of these.

1. We must chew our food properly before swallowing it.
2. We should not exercise immediately after eating.
3. Fruits and vegetables should always be washed before eating.

E. Answer these questions in brief.

1. Why do we need food?
2. What is the role of saliva?
3. What is the function of large intestine?

F. Answer these questions in detail.

1. What is digestion? Which organ system in our body digests food? Name the various organs connected with this system.
2. What is the role of the small intestine in digesting food?

G. Out of the box!

Find out why we should not take a bath immediately after eating a heavy meal.

H. Picture Talk

1. Label the organs of the digestive system.

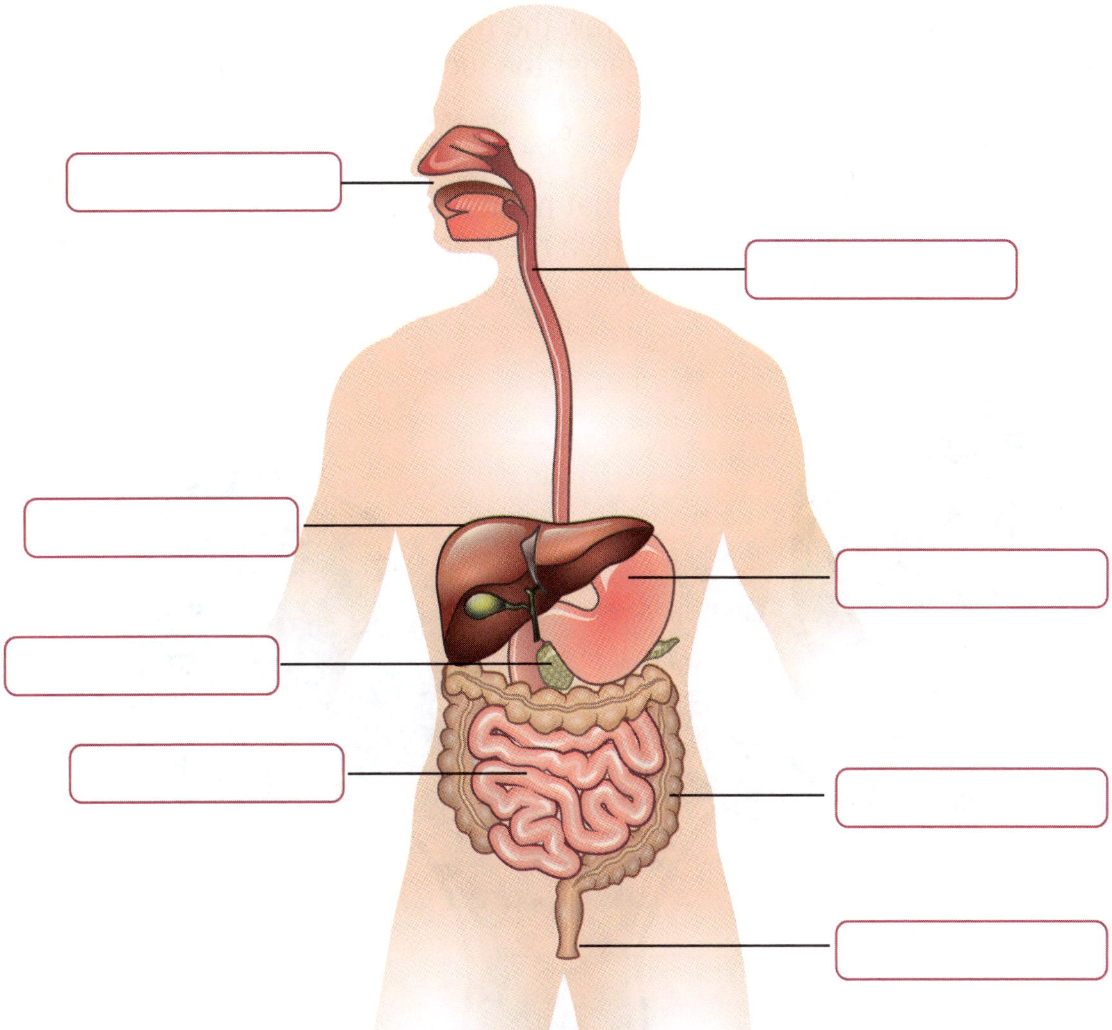

2. Look at the pictures given below. Circle those pictures that show healthy habits related to digestion.

Washing hands before eating

Eating pizza all the times

Eating fresh fruits

Skills Enrichment ZONE

A. 21 CS Creativity and Innovation, Life Skills | HQ How Similar are We | IF | AI | CC Integration with Social Studies

Find out the names of the famous food or dishes from any eight states of India. For example, *Singju* from Manipur. Draw the map of India on a chart paper and write down the name of the food against the location of the state.

B. 21 CS Critical Thinking, Life Skills | HQ Knowing My Needs | CC Integration with English

3 GOOD HEALTH AND WELL-BEING

Suppose you are walking on a road that heads to the food habits shown in the picture given below. Which road would you choose and why? Write a short note on your choice in your diary.

C. 21 CS Creativity and Innovation, Life Skills | HQ Living in an Interconnected Society | AI

2 ZERO HUNGER | 12 RESPONSIBLE CONSUMPTION AND PRODUCTION

Make a poster on one of the following topics.

1. Waste not, want not!
2. Eat healthy, live long!

What is the importance of making such posters? Share your thoughts with your classmates.

8 Circulatory and Excretory Systems

Prior Knowledge

In the previous classes, I have learnt that

- Many organs work together to form organ systems.
- Different organ systems perform different functions in body.

Learning Objectives

In this chapter, I will learn about:

- Circulatory system
- Excretory system

Let's Get Going

Look at these pictures. Write the names of the organs and the organ systems they belong to.

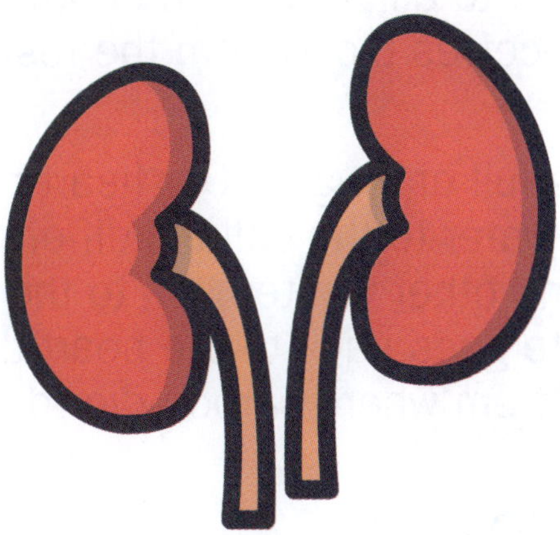

Organ: __________

Organ system: __________

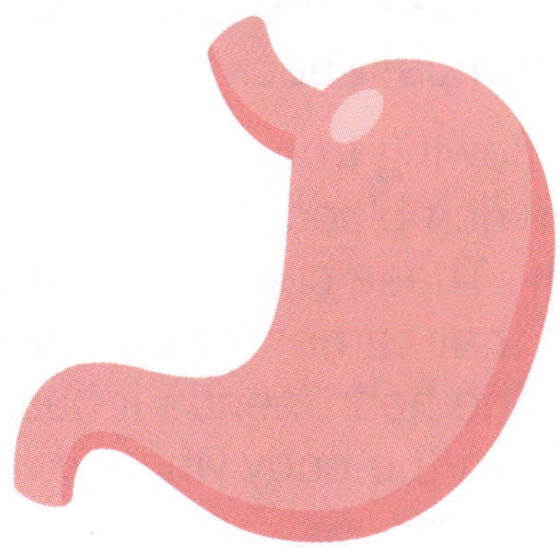

Organ: __________

Organ system: __________

We have already learnt that many organ systems in our body work together to enable it to function smoothly. In this chapter, let us learn more about two of the organ systems in the human body—the circulatory system and the excretory system.

CIRCULATORY SYSTEM

The circulatory system includes the **heart**, **blood** and **blood vessels**.

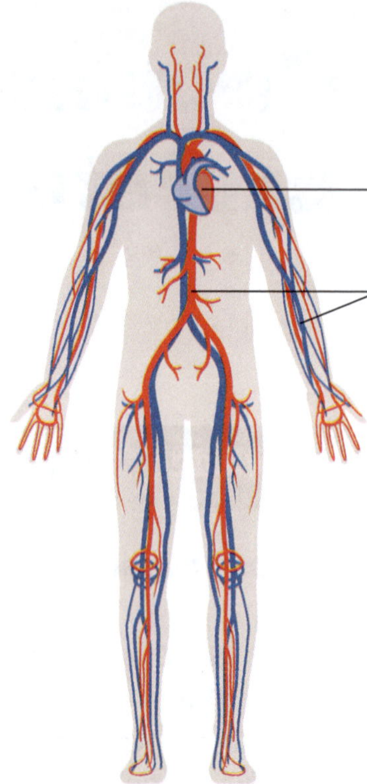

Circulatory system

Blood and blood vessels

When oxygen we breathe in through the nose passes into the lungs and then into the blood, the circulatory system starts its work. Blood is a red-coloured **fluid** that carries oxygen, nutrients and waste products and moves through thin tubes called **blood vessels**.

There are three types of blood vessels.

Arteries: These carry blood from the heart to other parts of the body.

Veins: These carry blood from other parts of the body back to the heart.

Capillaries: These are very fine branches of arteries that join together to form veins.

My Dictionary

fluid: a substance that is able to flow and change its shape easily

Heart

Our **heart** is like a pump. The left side of our heart receives blood from our lungs and pumps it to all parts of the body through the blood vessels. The right side of our heart receives blood from the rest of the body and pumps it back to the lungs.

The blood flowing from our lungs to the heart is full of oxygen. Our heart pumps this oxygen-rich blood along with nutrients and water to the cells in different parts of the body. These cells pass carbon dioxide and other waste back to the blood. This blood that carries carbon dioxide and waste goes back to the heart through the veins. The heart sends it back to the lungs from where carbon dioxide is released from the body when we breathe out.

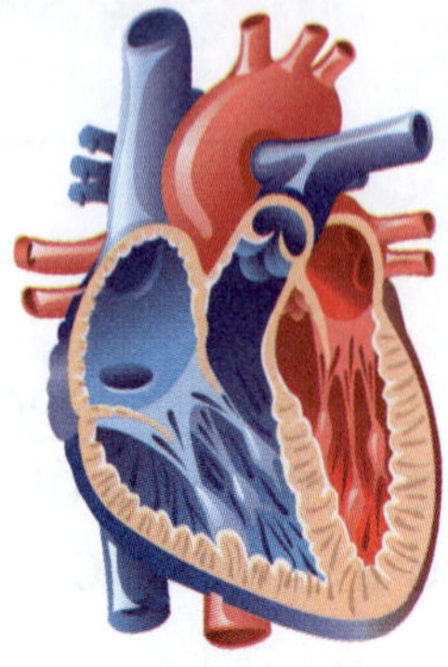
Heart

Real World

Your pulse is the throbbing of the arteries as blood moves through them. It shows the number of times your heart beats in one minute.

Let's Try

Sit down and put the index and the middle finger of your right hand on the wrist of your left hand. Press the fingers down slightly. What do you feel?

- Take a stopwatch and check your pulse. ________________ times
- Do spot jogging for one minute and count your pulse again. ________________ times

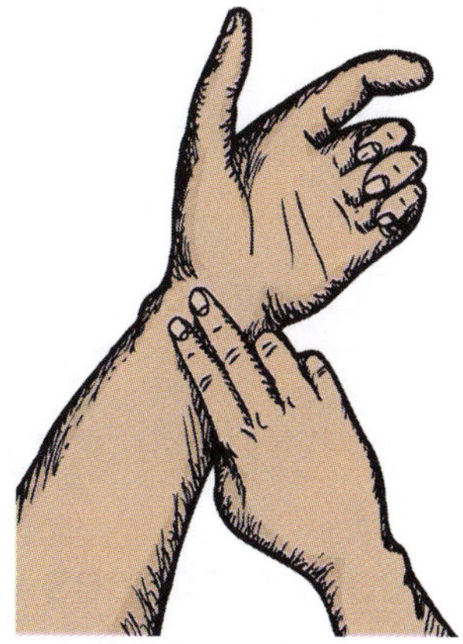

Do you find any change in the pulse rate?

When we exercise, our pulse rate goes up as the blood rushes to the muscles to provide extra energy for the physical activity. So, our heart rate also increases.

Can you think of any other time when your pulse rate goes up?

See how our circulatory system works.

1. When we breathe in, oxygen-rich air enters the blood from the lungs and is carried to the heart.
2. Heart pumps the oxygen-rich blood to other parts of the body.
3. Blood transports oxygen to different body parts. It also collects waste and carbon dioxide through the capillaries.
4. Blood returns to the heart with carbon dioxide.
5. Heart pumps the carbon dioxide-rich blood to the lungs where carbon dioxide is removed and more oxygen is added.

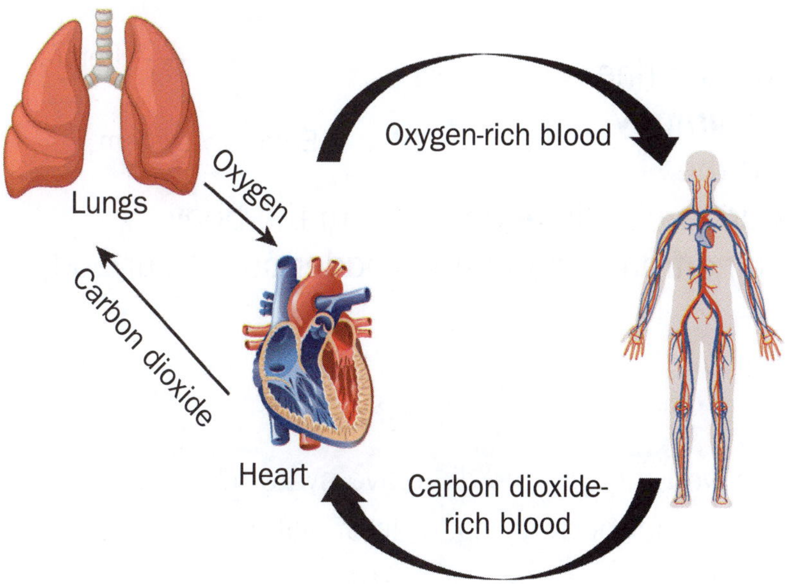

Working of circulatory system

Real World

Our heart is the size of our fist. It is an organ that never rests in our entire life. It works even when we are asleep.

Tech Updates

Robotic surgery is a type of surgical procedure that is done by robotic systems. In such surgeries, the doctor uses small instruments that fit into the patient's body through a series of tiny holes or incisions.

Knowledge Check

Fill in the blanks.

1. ______________, ______________ and ______________ make up the circulatory system.
2. ______________ carry blood from the heart to other parts of the body.
3. ______________ carry blood from other parts of the body to the heart.
4. Removal of carbon dioxide from blood takes place in the ______________.

EXCRETORY SYSTEM

Our body produces waste products such as sweat, urine and carbon dioxide. These wastes have to be removed regularly from our body. The removal of the waste from our body is carried out by the organs of the excretory system.

Sweat is given out through the pores in our skin. Carbon dioxide is released by the lungs and urine is released by the urinary system. Kidneys, ureter, urinary bladder and the urethra form the urinary system.

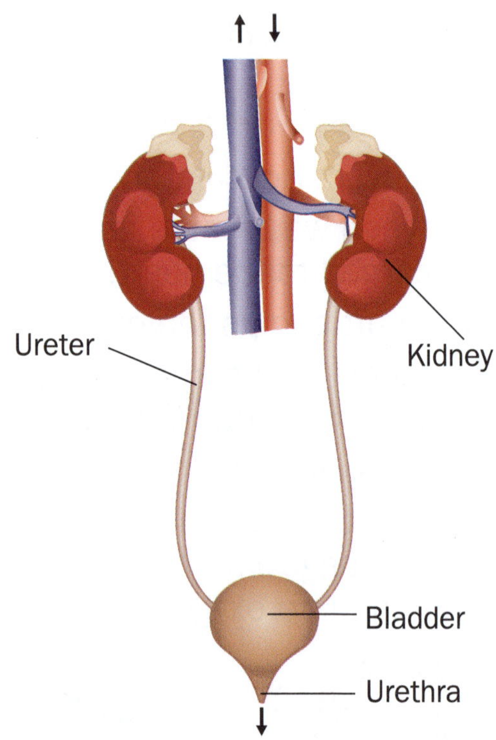

Excretory system

Kidneys are a pair of bean-shaped organs that filter harmful wastes and excess salt from the blood and form urine. From the kidneys, urine is carried to a sac-like bag called the **urinary bladder** by a pair of thin tubes called the **ureters**. The urinary bladder stores urine till it is released from the body. A thin tube called **urethra** lets the urine from the urinary bladder out of our body.

Real World

- The solid waste from our body is removed through the digestive system.
- We must drink plenty of water as 70% of our body is made up of water.

Concept Map

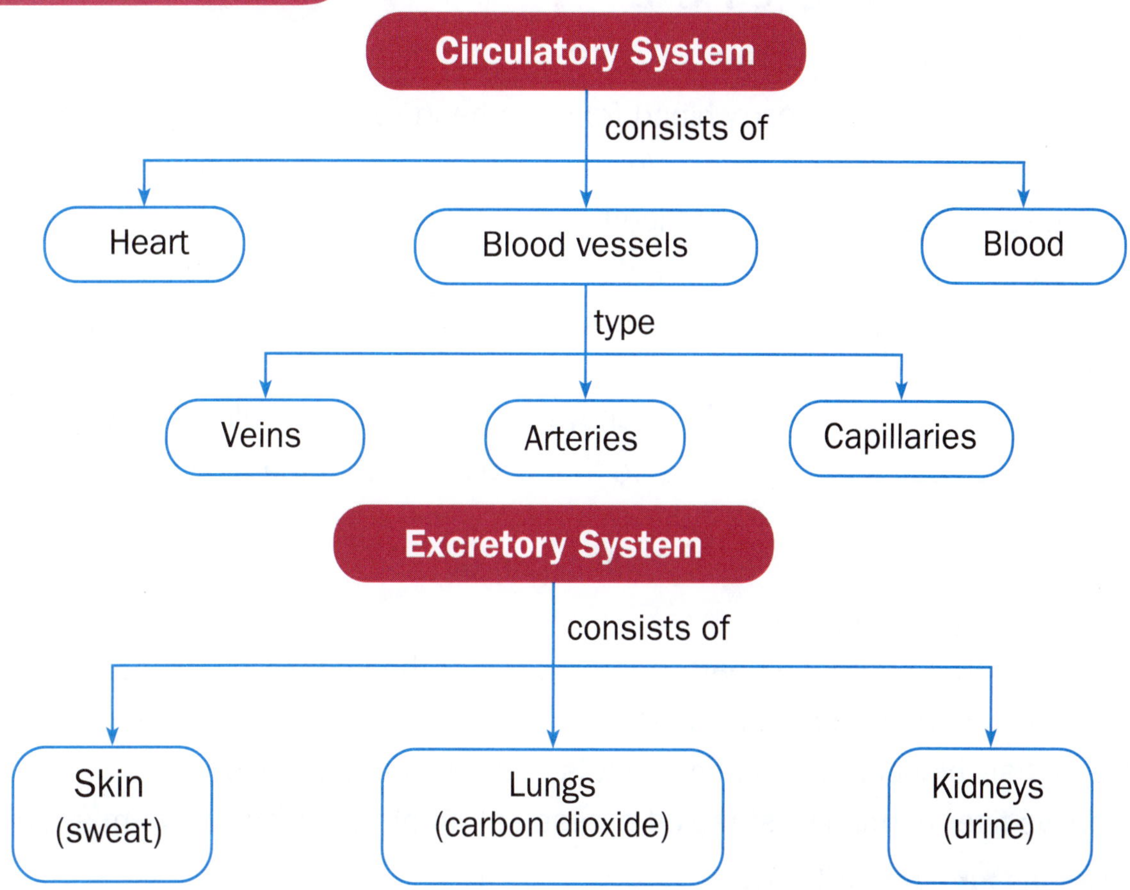

Summary

a. In this chapter, I have learnt that

- The circulatory system includes heart, blood and blood vessels.
- The three types of blood vessels are arteries, veins and capillaries.
- The heart pumps blood to all the parts of the body through blood vessels.
- Our body produces waste products such as sweat, urine and carbon dioxide.
- The excretory system helps remove wastes from our body.
- The organs of the excretory system are kidneys, lungs and skin.

b. I can do the following:

- Name the organs of the circulatory and excretory systems
- Describe the functioning of the circulatory and excretory systems
- Differentiate the three kinds of blood vessels
- Count my pulse rate
- Feel the difference between the pulse rate when I am resting and after exercise
- Identify and label parts of the circulatory and excretory systems

Practice ZONE

A. Choose the correct option.

1. ________________ carry blood from the heart to other parts of the body.

    a. Arteries   b. Veins   c. Capillaries

2. ________________ pumps blood.

    a. Heart   b. Kidney   c. Urethra

3. ________________ are the bean-shaped organs that filter waste from the blood.

    a. Heart   b. Kidneys   c. Blood vessels

4. ________________ is the waste that is filtered from the blood by the kidneys.

    a. Salt   b. Carbon dioxide   c. Sweat

B. Write T for true or F for false.

1. Blood is carried from the heart to other parts of the body by the veins.
2. Capillaries reunite to form arteries.
3. The urinary bladder stores urine till it is released from the body.
4. Kidneys filter harmful wastes and excess salt from the blood and form sweat.

C. Give reasons for each of these.

1. Heart is like a pump.
2. We cannot survive without the excretory system.

D. Answer these questions in brief.

1. What are the different organs of the circulatory system?
2. List the three types of blood vessels.
3. How are arteries different from veins?
4. Name any three waste products formed in the body.
5. Name the organs of the excretory system.

E. Answer these questions in detail.

1. What are the functions of the different organs of the excretory system? Explain.
2. Explain how blood travels through different parts of the body, starting from lungs and back to the lungs.

F. Out of the box!

Lekha goes out for jogging every morning. She feels her heart beats faster while jogging. Can you explain why?

G. Picture Talk

1. Label the diagram.

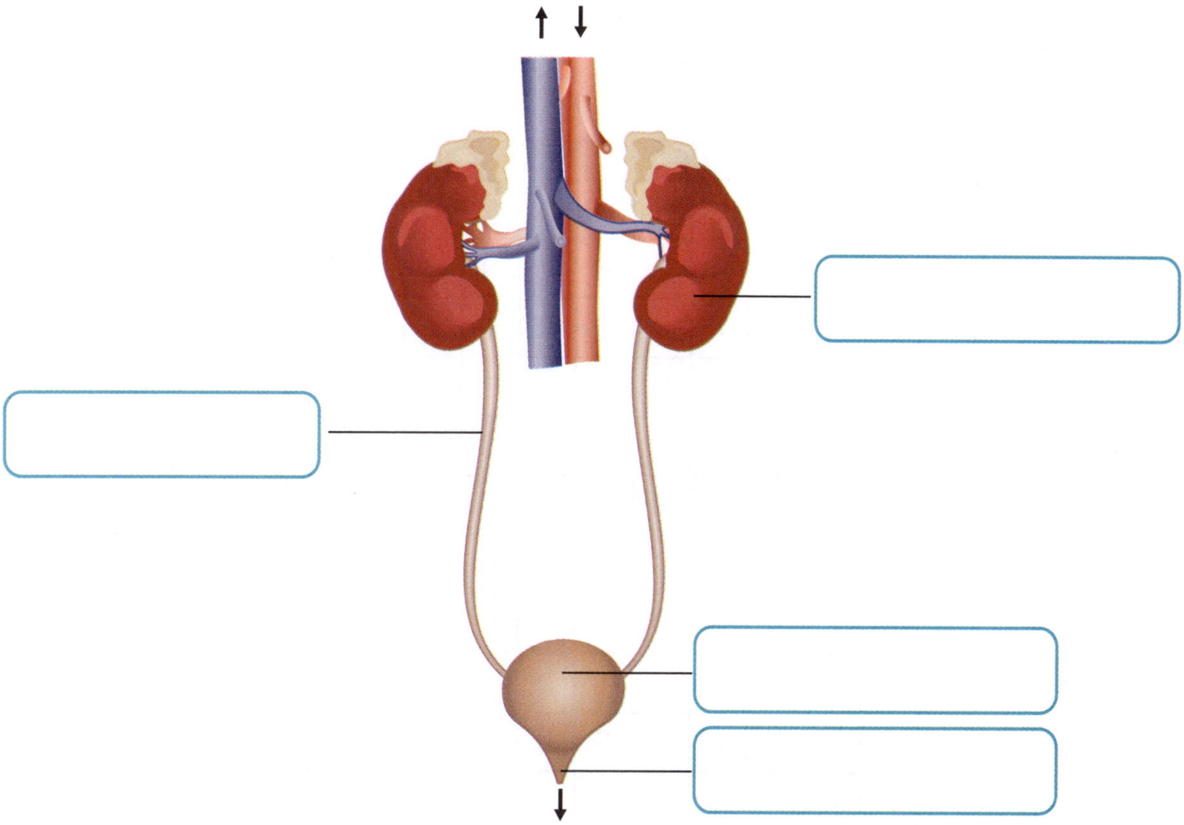

2. Look at the given picture and answer the following questions.

   a. What is this instrument called?
   b. What is it used for?
   c. Name the person who invented it.

Skills Enrichment ZONE

A. 21 CS Critical Thinking, Life Skills | HQ Knowing My Needs

3 GOOD HEALTH AND WELL-BEING

To keep your heart healthy:

- do yoga and pranayama (breathing exercises)
- eat healthy
- exercise regularly

Can you add more to the list?

B. 21 CS Critical Thinking, Information Literacy   CC Integration with English

Find the names of the specialists in the given wordsearch.

CARDIOLOGIST   UROLOGIST   DERMATOLOGIST   RADIOLOGIST
PATHOLOGIST   NEPHROLOGIST

<table>
<tr><td>O</td><td>W</td><td>N</td><td>E</td><td>P</td><td>H</td><td>R</td><td>O</td><td>L</td><td>O</td><td>G</td><td>I</td><td>S</td><td>T</td><td>N</td></tr>
<tr><td>T</td><td>B</td><td>R</td><td>K</td><td>C</td><td>G</td><td>M</td><td>V</td><td>O</td><td>Q</td><td>L</td><td>J</td><td>D</td><td>S</td><td>W</td></tr>
<tr><td>S</td><td>R</td><td>U</td><td>N</td><td>F</td><td>O</td><td>J</td><td>H</td><td>T</td><td>I</td><td>E</td><td>T</td><td>P</td><td>J</td><td>C</td></tr>
<tr><td>U</td><td>M</td><td>P</td><td>A</td><td>T</td><td>H</td><td>O</td><td>L</td><td>O</td><td>G</td><td>I</td><td>S</td><td>T</td><td>T</td><td>M</td></tr>
<tr><td>O</td><td>T</td><td>S</td><td>B</td><td>D</td><td>B</td><td>S</td><td>F</td><td>G</td><td>D</td><td>K</td><td>G</td><td>R</td><td>L</td><td>R</td></tr>
<tr><td>U</td><td>R</td><td>O</td><td>L</td><td>O</td><td>G</td><td>I</td><td>S</td><td>T</td><td>J</td><td>C</td><td>I</td><td>Z</td><td>N</td><td>D</td></tr>
<tr><td>P</td><td>K</td><td>B</td><td>Y</td><td>Y</td><td>S</td><td>K</td><td>S</td><td>Y</td><td>I</td><td>E</td><td>P</td><td>A</td><td>E</td><td>H</td></tr>
<tr><td>W</td><td>R</td><td>F</td><td>Y</td><td>S</td><td>C</td><td>K</td><td>U</td><td>Q</td><td>F</td><td>L</td><td>A</td><td>L</td><td>U</td><td>Z</td></tr>
<tr><td>W</td><td>H</td><td>P</td><td>R</td><td>A</td><td>D</td><td>I</td><td>O</td><td>L</td><td>O</td><td>G</td><td>I</td><td>S</td><td>T</td><td>D</td></tr>
<tr><td>A</td><td>Z</td><td>R</td><td>V</td><td>F</td><td>K</td><td>S</td><td>B</td><td>Q</td><td>M</td><td>H</td><td>L</td><td>G</td><td>Q</td><td>J</td></tr>
<tr><td>T</td><td>P</td><td>R</td><td>X</td><td>V</td><td>H</td><td>T</td><td>O</td><td>Z</td><td>N</td><td>G</td><td>L</td><td>C</td><td>H</td><td>Q</td></tr>
<tr><td>Z</td><td>B</td><td>V</td><td>S</td><td>D</td><td>Z</td><td>Y</td><td>A</td><td>W</td><td>V</td><td>M</td><td>F</td><td>W</td><td>V</td><td>B</td></tr>
<tr><td>D</td><td>E</td><td>R</td><td>M</td><td>A</td><td>T</td><td>O</td><td>L</td><td>O</td><td>G</td><td>I</td><td>S</td><td>T</td><td>U</td><td>B</td></tr>
<tr><td>N</td><td>G</td><td>X</td><td>O</td><td>K</td><td>O</td><td>O</td><td>X</td><td>Z</td><td>R</td><td>Q</td><td>B</td><td>G</td><td>P</td><td>J</td></tr>
<tr><td>C</td><td>A</td><td>R</td><td>D</td><td>I</td><td>O</td><td>L</td><td>O</td><td>G</td><td>I</td><td>S</td><td>T</td><td>M</td><td>W</td><td>D</td></tr>
</table>

C. 21 CS Communication   CC Integration with English   IF

Add the word 'heart' and complete the phrases. Find out the meaning of each phrase in English and in your mother tongue.

1. Have a ________________
2. ________________ in my mouth
3. Close to my ________________
4. Lose ________________
5. ________________ and soul

Worksheet 3

STEAM CHALLENGE

Trisha's father took her to their family doctor for her regular check-up. The doctor used an instrument to check her heart rate. Being a curious child, Trisha asked the doctor about the instrument. The doctor told her that the instrument is called a stethoscope. It is used to listen the heartbeat.

On arriving back home, Trisha thought of having her own stethoscope. Can you help her in making a stethoscope?

What is the challenge?

What supplies do you need?

IDEA 1

IDEA 2

What worked or did not work for you?

How can you improve it?

9 Soil

Prior Knowledge

In the previous classes, I have learnt that

- Plants grow in soil.
- Many living creatures are found in soil.
- We should take steps to conserve soil.

Learning Objectives

In this chapter, I will learn about:

- Soil formation
- Soil composition
- Types of soil
- Soil profile
- Soil erosion
- Soil conservation

Let's Get Going

Help the earthworm to reach the top of the soil.

Soil is essential for life on the Earth. It covers the Earth's surface. Plants and trees grow in it and provide food for most living things. It is the home for many living beings, insects and animals. It is made up of fine particles of rocks, minerals, sand, clay, humus along with air and water.

Talk About

Name the different layers of components present in the soil.

SOIL FORMATION

Soil formation is a long and slow process. Over hundreds of years, large pieces of rocks are broken down into smaller pieces by the actions of rain, heat and wind till some become powdery and form soil. This process of breaking down of rocks is called **weathering**.

You must have seen the *peepal* and banyan plantlets growing from cracks in buildings. As they grow bigger, their roots crack the walls. Similarly, plants grow in the cracks of rocks. The roots of these plants push down and break the rocks into smaller pieces. Some animals also burrow and crack rocks. Over a period, the rocks break into finer powder called sand. The remains of dead animals and plants get mixed in the soil and form humus. Humus makes the soil fertile.

SOIL COMPOSITION

Soil is made up of gravel, sand, clay particles, humus, water, air, minerals and **microorganisms** such as bacteria. Let us learn more about the basic components of soil.

1. **Rock materials:** Gravel, sand, clay, silt and pebbles
2. **Organic material:** Derived from plants and humus
3. **Air:** We have already studied in Class 3 that soil contains air. The plant roots and other organisms require oxygen for breathing. Plants also need nitrogen and carbon dioxide for growth.
4. **Water:** Water is required by plants and other creatures living in the soil.
5. **Microorganisms and living things:** Soil has many living things like earthworms, fungi and bacteria that help in the formation of humus.

My Dictionary

microorganisms: organisms that are very small to be seen with naked eye and can be seen only under a microscope

Your Task

Be a soil detective!
In groups, go to different parts of your school park or garden with a magnifying glass and dig the soil and observe. You will be surprised to see the creatures in the soil. Discuss with your friends.

Types of soil

Soil is classified into five different types based on its particle size, texture and colour.

- **Gravel:** Gravel consists of a large number of tiny stones that allow water to pass easily. Thus, it does not hold water.
- **Sand:** Sand is light and dry with a rough texture. It does not hold water.
- **Clay:** Clay particles are very fine and closely packed. Clay holds water and it is sticky when wet.
- **Loam:** Loam is a mixture of sand, clay and humus. Thus, the size of its particles varies.
- **Silt:** Silt is a fertile soil that is brought down by rivers. Silt particles are smaller than sand particles.

Gravel

Sand

Clay

Loam

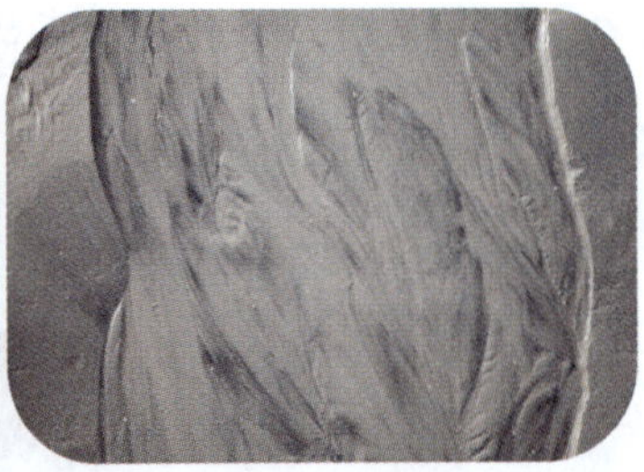

Silt

Real World

- The amount of sand, clay and silt gives the different soil types their textures.
- Soil may be red in colour due to the presence of iron in it.

Knowledge Check

Fill in the blanks.

1. Different types of soil are __________, __________, __________, __________ and __________.
2. __________ is the process of breaking down of soil.
3. __________ is the remains of dead animals and plants that make the soil fertile.
4. __________ and __________ are microorganisms found in the soil.

SOIL PROFILE

Soil profile refers to the layers of soil that we see when we dig downwards from the surface of the Earth. There are three layers of soil: topsoil, subsoil and bedrock.

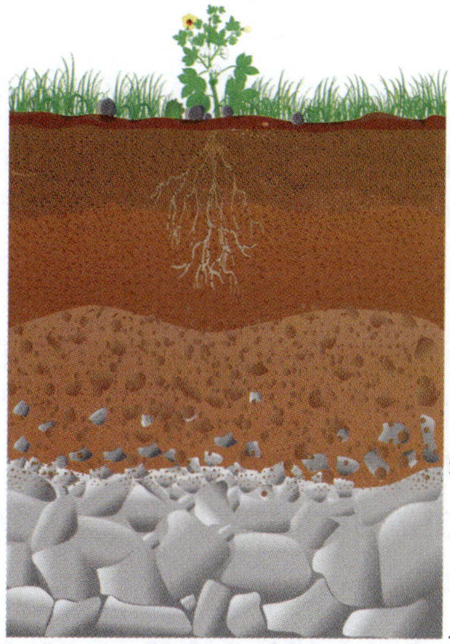

Soil profile

Topsoil

Topsoil is the uppermost layer of soil that contains different types of particles such as sand, gravel, humus, air and water. Plants grow on the topsoil.

Subsoil

The middle layer of soil is called the subsoil. It is right below the topsoil. Subsoil is rich in minerals. It contains broken pieces of rocks. It has water and very little humus.

Bedrock

The bottom layer of soil is called the bedrock. It is situated quite deep inside the Earth and is largely made up of rocks. There is not much water present here.

Soil profile is different in different areas. The climate of the area and the time taken for the formation of soil affect the soil profile.

SOIL EROSION

The wearing away of topsoil by the actions of wind, rain or human activity is called soil erosion.

Soil erosion is a natural process. However, it becomes a problem when human activity causes it to occur faster than it occurs under natural conditions. Overcultivation, deforestation, mechanized farming (usage of machines on the farms) and overgrazing by animals hasten soil erosion.

RESULTS OF SOIL EROSION

Soil erosion results in:

- infertile land
- **desertification**
- **devastating** floods

My Dictionary

- **desertification:** the process by which fertile land turns into desert
- **devastating:** destroying

SOIL CONSERVATION

Prevention of soil from erosion is called soil conservation. Here are some ways we can conserve soil, and how it can help us.

- Plant more trees in place of the ones being cut down. Trees can be planted in areas that have few or none. Plants help to hold the soil in place; they also slow the flow of water down a slope. Trees also help break the force of rain drops falling on the soil.
- Avoid overgrazing by cattle. This means that we should not allow the cattle to graze in the same area for a long period of time.
- Practise crop rotation by growing different kinds of crops on the same field in different seasons. Different crops require different kinds of nutrients. Thus, crop rotation maintains the fertility of soil.
- Build embankments (walls of stone or Earth made to keep the water in the river) along the riverbanks. This prevents the fertile topsoil from getting carried away during floods. This also saves the crops from getting damaged.
- Stop the soil in hilly areas from flowing down by creating terrace fields. This prevents the soil from being carried down the hill during heavy rainfall.

Planting trees prevents soil erosion.

Avoid overgrazing

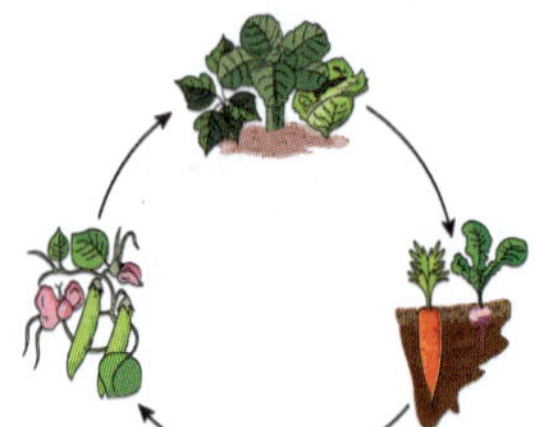

Crop rotation

River embankment

Terrace farming

Let's Try

Take two ice cream cups and fill them with soil. In one cup, plant a tuft of grass with roots. Plant a tuft with the roots cut-off in the other cup.
Press down both plants into the soil. After a few days, lift plant A (with roots) and plant B (with no roots). Which one holds the soil? Discuss your observation.

Tech Updates

Hydroponics is a new type of soil-free agriculture. In this method, plants are grown in a mixture of water, nutrients and oxygen.

Concept Map

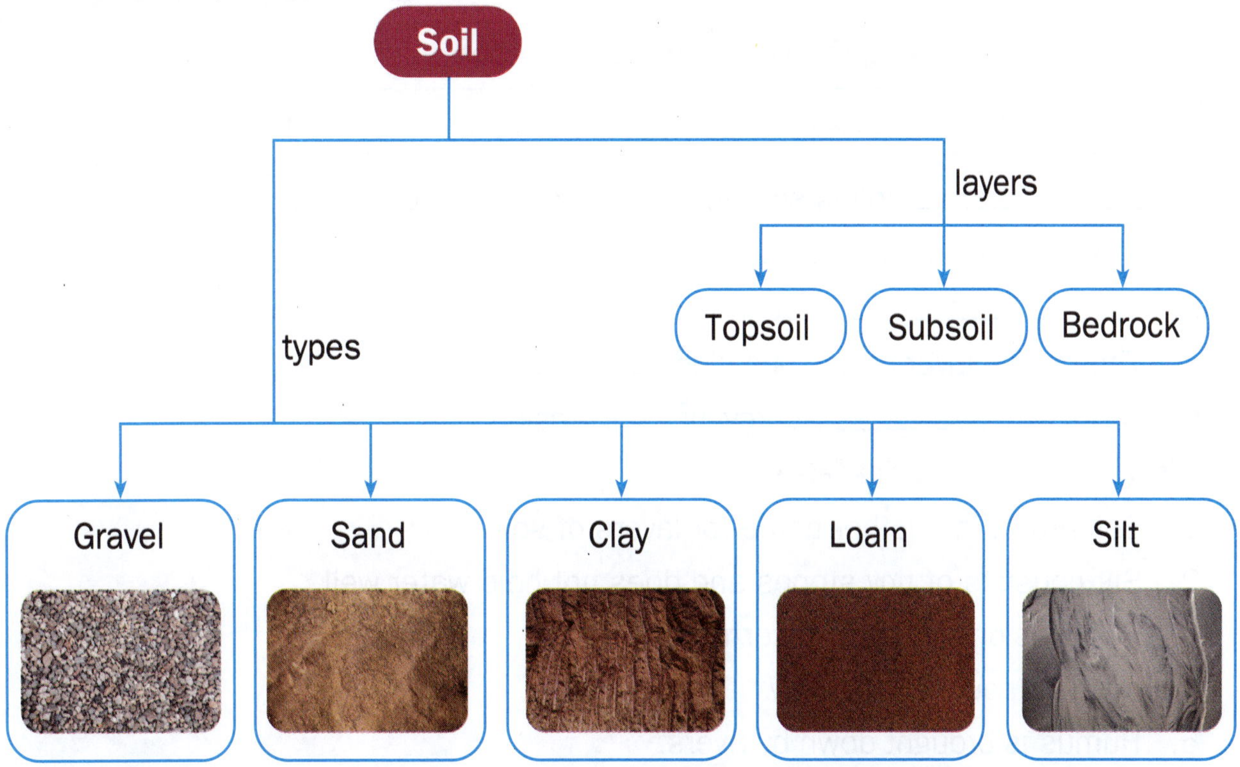

Summary

a. In this chapter, I have learnt that

- The process of breaking down of rocks is called weathering.
- The basic components of soil are rocks, remains of plants and animals, air, water and microorganisms.
- The different types of soil are gravel, sand, clay, loam and silt.
- The three layers of soil are topsoil, subsoil and bedrock.
- Wearing away of topsoil by the action of wind, rain or human activities is called soil erosion.
- Soil erosion leads to infertile land, desertification and devastating floods.
- Prevention of soil from erosion is called soil conservation.

b. I can do the following:

- State the process of formation of soil
- List the components of soil
- Identify and name the types of soil
- Define soil erosion and suggest ways to prevent it

Practice ZONE

A. Fill in the blanks using the words given in the box.

embankments	subsoil	clayey	humus	sand

1. ____________ soil is smooth and sticky when wet.
2. Topsoil is rich in ____________.
3. ____________ has a rough texture.
4. The middle layer of soil is called ____________.
5. Building ____________ prevents soil erosion.

B. Write T for true or F for false.

1. Soil profile is another name for layers of soil.
2. Silt consists of tiny stones and does not hold water well.
3. Soil erosion makes land fertile.
4. Animals need soil to grow.
5. Humus is brought down by rivers.

C. Give two examples for each of these.

1. Microorganisms found in the soil
2. Human activities that lead to soil erosion
3. Particles found in topsoil

D. Give reasons for each of the these.

1. An earthworm is called a friend of the farmer.
2. Potters use clay to make mud pots and not sand.
3. Hardly any trees grow in deserts.

E. Answer these questions in brief.

1. Why is soil important for us?
2. What is soil made up of?
3. List different types of soils.
4. What are the disadvantages of soil erosion?
5. What is crop rotation?

F. Answer these questions in detail.

1. Explain the process of soil formation from rocks.
2. What is soil profile? Explain three layers of soil?

3. What is soil erosion? How does it happen?
4. What is the conservation of soil? Write different ways to conserve soil.
5. Which layer of soil is important for the growth of plants? Why?

G. Out of the box!

Ravi planted a sapling in a pot. He learnt that plants need water. Therefore, he watered the plant 3 times in a day. In a few days, the plant died. Why do you think this happened?

H. Picture Talk

1. Label the given diagram.

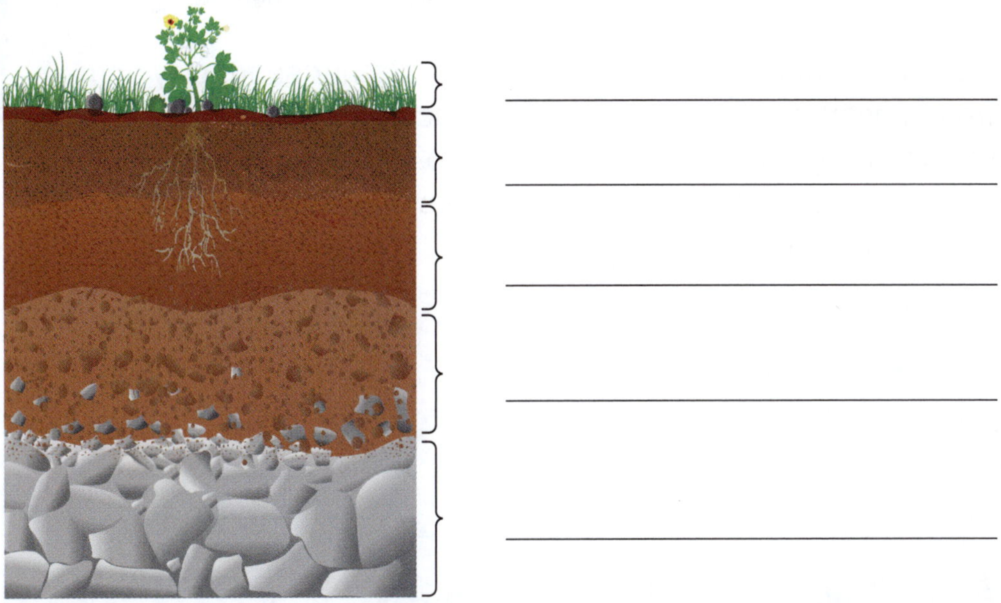

2. Look at the given picture and answer the questions that follow.
   a. Why are the roots exposed?
   b. What do you think has happened to the soil?
   c. Where do you think this picture is taken?

Skills Enrichment ZONE

A. 21 CS Critical Thinking, Information Literacy | HQ Coexisting with Nature | CC Integration with Social Studies

11 SUSTAINABLE CITIES AND COMMUNITIES

We know that human beings first settled down along the banks of rivers. They built their cities and did farming in these areas. Why do you think they chose river banks for settlement? Find out the names of four such civilizations and the places where they flourished.

B. 21 CS Collaboration, Life Skills | HQ Cooperation and Collaborative Living | EL | CC Integration with English

15 LIFE ON LAND

With the help of your elders, take three pots. Gather sand, clay and loam from a nearby park and put them in each pot. Sow a seed in each pot and water them every day. What do you observe after 7–10 days? Share the findings with your classmates and write a short note on it in your diary.

Sand

Clay

Loam

C. 21 CS Information Literacy, Life Skills | HQ Coexisting with Nature

13 CLIMATE ACTION

It takes around 2,000 years of natural activities and processes to make 10 centimetres of fertile soil. Every year, around 24 billion tonnes of topsoil is lost due to soil erosion and other agricultural practices. Find out the ways by which you can help conserve soil.

10 Solids, Liquids and Gases

Prior Knowledge

In the previous classes, I have learnt that

- Things around us can be grouped as solids, liquids or gases.
- Water exists in all three forms.

Learning Objectives

In this chapter, I will learn about:

- States of matter
- Changes in states of matter
- Dissolving solids in water

Let's Get Going

The containers are filled with items in different states of matter. Do you know these states of matter? Write the states of matter in the space provided below each container.

Look around the classroom. What do you see? There are things such as desks, chairs and blackboards that are of different shapes, sizes, colours and textures.

You have already studied in Class 3 that anything that has mass and occupies space is called **matter**. Animals, plants, stones, air and water are some examples of matter. However, light and shadow are not matter. Do you know why?

Talk About

Which item weighs more? The ball or the bottle? Why?

The **mass** of an object is the amount of matter it contains. We use a weighing balance to compare the masses of objects.

The amount of space that matter occupies is called its **volume**.

STATES OF MATTER

Matter can exist in three states: **solids**, **liquids** and **gases**. An ice cube is solid, water is liquid and the steam coming out of a kettle is gas.

Your Task

1. Fill a glass with water right up to the top. Drop a small rubber ball in it. What do you see? Explain your observation.

   ____

   ____

   ____

   ____

2. Can you identify the states of matter in the picture?

   ____

   ____

   ____

   ____

What is matter made up of?

Matter is made up of tiny particles.

The form of these particles remains the same in all states of matter. It is only the arrangement of the particles that changes in each state. Depending on the arrangement of the particles, there is more space or less space between the particles.

Solids

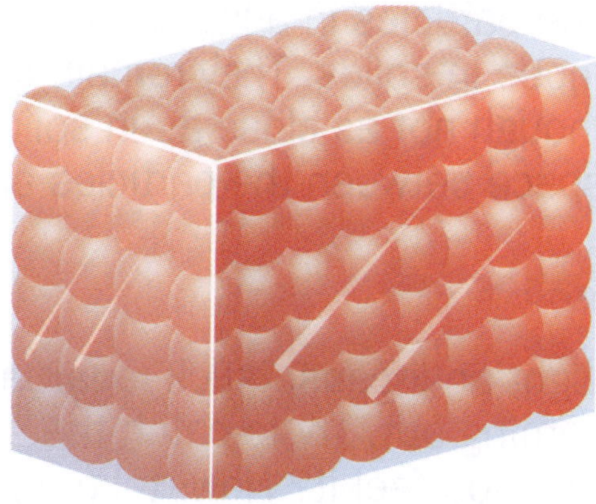

Particles in solids

Take a wooden dice and observe it carefully. What is its shape? How does it feel? Now, place the dice in a bowl. Does it change shape? Toss it in the air. Do you notice any change in its shape or size? Squeeze the wooden dice with your hands. Can you make it smaller? No, it does not change its shape or size. This is because the wooden dice is a solid.

A solid always has the same shape, whether it is on a table or in a bowl. We can say that all solids have a **definite shape**. Another characteristic of a solid object is that it always takes up the same amount of space. Therefore, a solid has a **definite volume**.

In solids, particles are packed very closely. So, solids are hard to touch and have a fixed shape, size and volume. A book, eraser and ball are some examples of solids.

Real World

Sand is solid because each grain that it is made up of is a very small solid that can hold its shape.

Book

Eraser

Ball

Liquids

What happens when you pour water from a bottle into a glass, a bowl and a dish?

You will see that the shape of water is different in each container. This is because water is a liquid.

So, we can say that a liquid has no shape of its own. It takes the shape of the container it is poured into. The volume of a liquid does not change whether it is poured into a glass, a dish or a bowl. Water, milk, oil and juice are some examples of liquids.

Your Task

Name any three liquids used in cooking.

Water

Juice

Milk

Remember

Liquids always flow from a higher level to a lower level.

The particles in a liquid are more loosely packed than those in solids. They remain close to one another, though not as close as in solids. This results in more space between the particles and allows the liquid to flow.

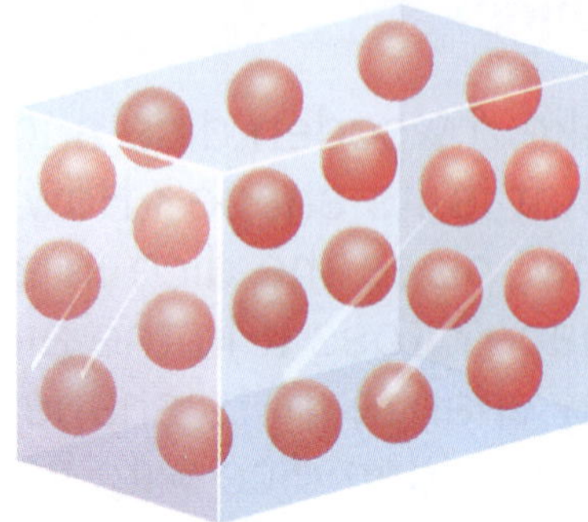

Particles in liquid

Gases

Light an incense stick (*agarbatti*). You will see smoke coming out. Try to catch the smoke. What happens? Can you feel it? Now, take a glass tumbler and cover the incense stick with it. You will notice that the smoke spreads and fills up the glass.

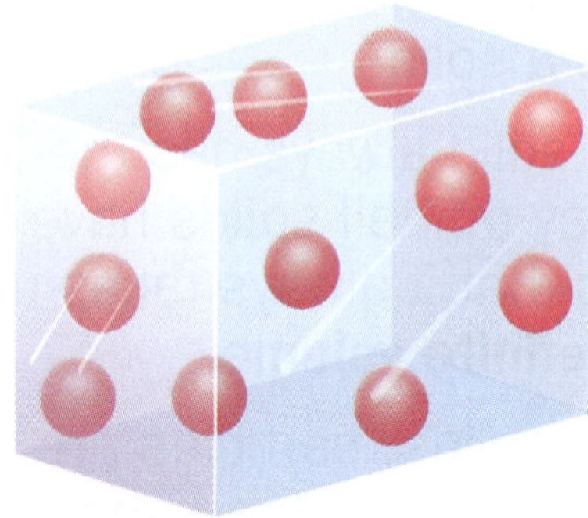

Particles in gas

Breathe into your palm. Do you feel the air?

Gases, such as air and smoke, have no fixed shape and volume. They can fill up the entire space or be **compressed** into a smaller area. Gases flow to take the shape of the container they are in. The particles in a gas are loosely packed and are far apart. Thus, they can move about freely to fill up any space. Therefore, when we spray room freshener in the corner of a room, it spreads quickly to fill the entire room.

My Dictionary

compressed: squeezed

Incense stick

Balloon

Real World

Air is a mixture of gases with nitrogen being the most dominant component, followed by oxygen.

Knowledge Check

Write T for True or F for false.

1. Gases can be squeezed.
2. Air is matter.
3. In a solid, the particles are far apart.
4. The mass and volume of an object hold the same meaning.

CHANGES IN STATES OF MATTER

Matter can change from one state to another on heating or cooling.

Put a tray of water in the freezer. It turns into ice after a few hours. Water changes from a liquid state to solid state on cooling. This process is called **freezing**.

Take out the tray of ice and keep it outside for some time. What do you see? You will notice that the ice changes back into water. The process of a solid changing into a liquid on heating is called **melting**.

Ask an adult to heat some water in a pan. You will notice water vapour or steam rising from the pan in some time. The process of water changing into water vapour on heating is called **evaporation**.

When we hold a cold plate against the steam or water vapour, we see water droplets forming on the surface of the plate. The steam changes into water on coming in contact with the cold surface. The process of a gas changing into a liquid on cooling is called **condensation**.

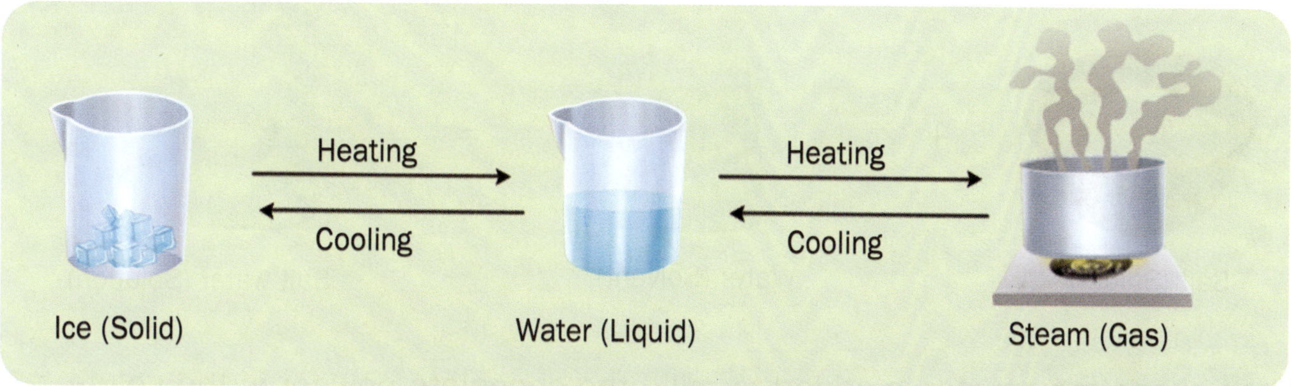

Changes in states of matter

Real World

Boiling is the process in which a substance changes its state from liquid to gas at a definite temperature (boiling point). The boiling point of water is 100 °C.

Your Task

Take water in a glass and mark its level.

Take some salt and add it to water. Stir or heat it.

What happens to the salt?

The salt disappears. Also, there is no change in the level of water with the addition of salt. Now, taste the water. It is salty. Why does this happen?

DISSOLVING SOLIDS IN WATER

The process in which a solid or a gas completely mixes or dissolves in a liquid is called **dissolution**.
Solids such as sugar and salt completely dissolve in water. The solid that dissolves in water is called a **solute**. The liquid in which the solid dissolves is called the **solvent**. The liquid that we get after a solid dissolves in a liquid is called a **solution**.

Real World

Sea creatures survive in water by breathing the oxygen present in water.

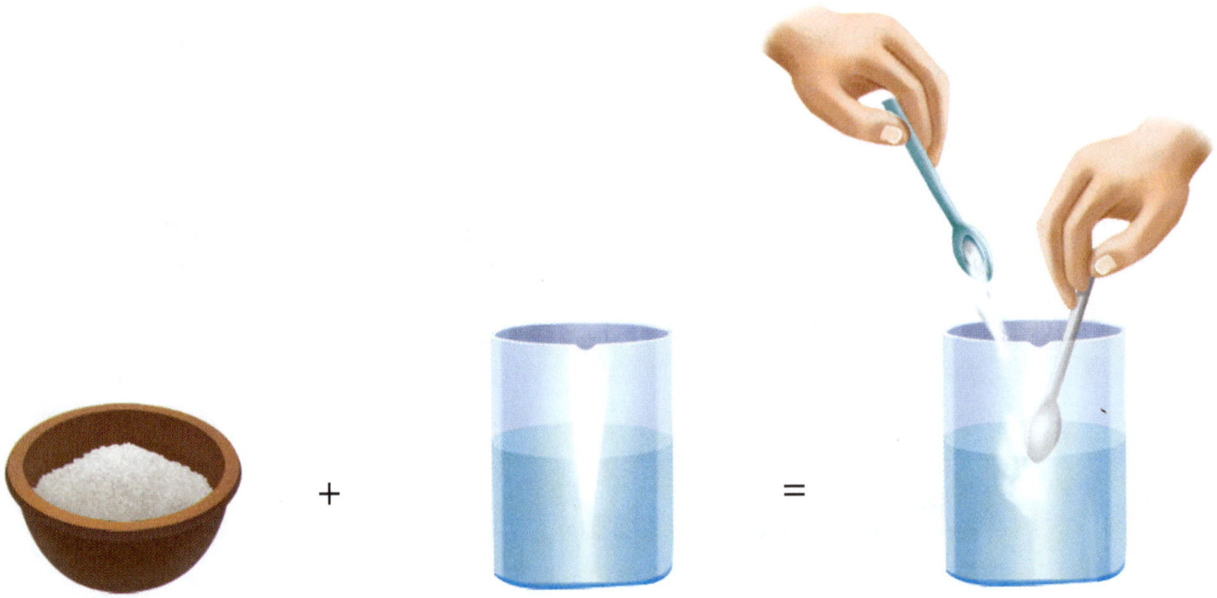

Salt (Solute) + Water (Solvent) = Salt water (Solution)

When chocolate powder is added to milk, the chocolate powder is the solute, milk is the solvent and chocolate milk is the solution.

We know that the particles in a liquid are loosely packed, leaving a lot of space between the particles. The solute particles break down into tinier particles when added to the solvent and get uniformly (evenly) distributed among the particles of the solvent. Thus, leaving no change in the level of water.

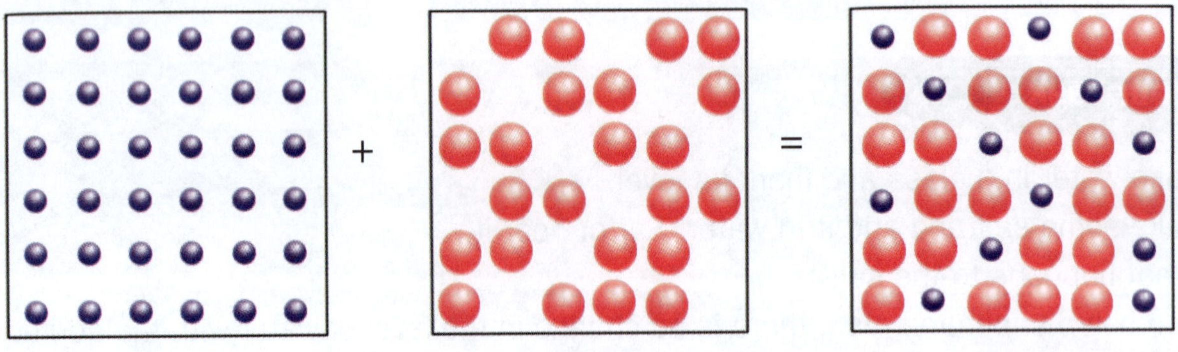

Solute + Solvent = Solution

Concept Map

Matter

states

Solid
- Fixed shape
- Fixed volume
- Closely packed particles

example: Football

Liquid
- No fixed shape
- Fixed volume
- Loosely packed particles

example: Water

Gas
- No fixed shape
- No fixed volume
- Freely moving particles

example: Steam

Summary

a. In this chapter, I have learnt that

- Matter is made up of tiny particles called particles.
- In solids, the particles are closely packed. So, solids are hard to touch and have a fixed shape, volume and size.
- In liquids, particles are loosely packed. So, liquids have fixed volume but no fixed shape.
- The particles in a gas are far apart. Hence, a gas has no fixed shape or volume.
- Matter can change from one state to another on heating or cooling.
- Solute dissolves in a solvent to give a solution.

b. I can do the following:

- Compare and contrast the three states of matter
- Define terms such as solute, solvent and solution
- Make solutions using different solutes and solvents

Practice ZONE

A. Choose the correct option.

1. ____________ state of matter has tightly packed particles.
   a. Solid b. Liquid c. Gas
2. ____________ state of matter is easily compressible.
   a. Solid b. Liquid c. Gas
3. ____________ is the process by which ice turns into water.
   a. Freezing b. Condensation c. Melting
4. ____________ is the measure of the amount of matter present in a substance.
   a. Mass b. Volume c. Shape

B. Write T for true or F for false.

1. Two objects cannot occupy the same space.
2. The intermolecular space in solids is more than that in liquids.
3. The process of a liquid changing into a solid is called freezing.
4. A liquid has a definite shape.

C. Fill in the blanks using the words given in the box.

solids	heating	solute	solution	evaporation	cooling

1. The space between the particles is the least in ______________ .
2. Matter can change from one state to another on ______________ or ______________.
3. The process of water changing into water vapour on heating is called ______________.
4. A ____________ dissolves in a solvent to form a ______________.

D. Give reasons for each of these.

1. We cannot compress a solid ball of metal.
2. Milk boils over but water does not.
3. Ice cream melts when left out on a table for some time.

E. Answer these questions in brief.

1. What makes it possible for liquids to flow?
2. When someone sprays a perfume in one room, how can a person in the next room smell it?
3. Define freezing and melting.

F. Answer these questions in detail.

1. What are the characteristics of gases? Explain them.
2. What will you see if you hold a cold plate over a steaming bowl of water? What is the reason behind your observations? What is this process called?

G. Out of the box!

1. All materials when melted expand in volume. However, when ice melts, the water at the same temperature occupies less volume. Why do you think this happens?
2. Why do you think a chapati swells up when cooked over flame?

H. Picture Talk

1. Label the diagram.

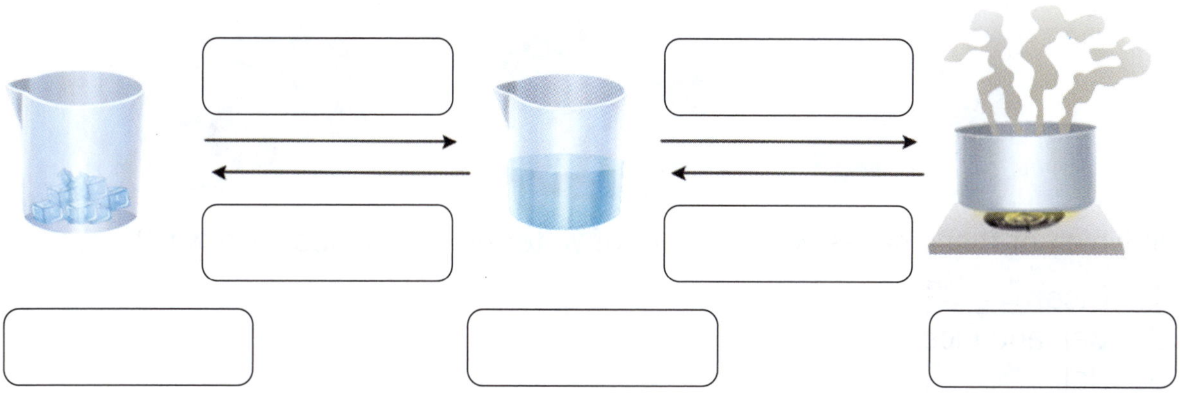

2. The liquid of a beaker was poured into a round shaped beaker as shown in the picture.
   The liquid in the beaker changes its ________________.
   a. mass b. shape c. volume

3. Look at the picture carefully. From where did the water come into the beaker?

Skills Enrichment ZONE

A. 21 CS Critical Thinking, Information Literacy | CC Integration with Mathematics

A beaker contains some water. The picture shows what happens to the level of water when different objects are dropped into it.

In which of these cases will the level of water be the highest and why?

1. Dice
2. Ball and dice
3. Ball

B. 21 CS Creativity and Innovation, Life Skills | HQ Happiness My Goal | AI

3 GOOD HEALTH AND WELL-BEING

Make a jelly pudding!

Ingredients:

- Packet of jelly crystals
- Warm water

Method:

- Place the jelly crystals in a bowl.
- Add warm water and stir well.
- Place the bowl in the refrigerator for four hours till the pudding sets.
- Garnish your pudding with nuts and fruits.

C. 21 CS Critical Thinking | HQ Harmony in Self

Rahul was playing in his room. Suddenly he felt the smell of his favourite food coming from the kitchen. He immediately went to the kitchen to taste it. Can you tell, how come Rahul got to know about his favourite food being cooked in the kitchen?

11 Force, Work and Energy

Prior Knowledge

In the previous classes, I have learnt that

- Any pull or push is called force.
- We use various machines in our daily life.
- Sun is the main source of energy on the Earth.

Learning Objectives

In this chapter, I will learn about:

- What can force do
- Types of force
- Work
- Simple machines
- Energy
- Sources of energy

Let's Get Going

Name these machines we use at home.

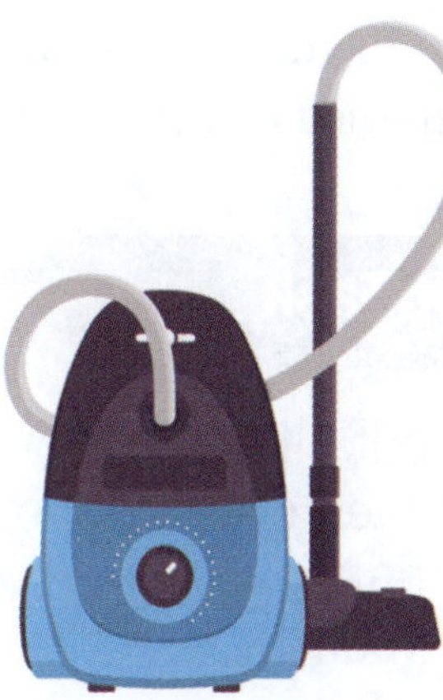

FORCE

We have learnt in Class 3 that force is a push, pull or twist acting on a body. To do any kind of work, we need to apply force. For example, we apply force when we push a trolley in a supermarket pull a drawer or squeeze a lemon.

Real World

To do any kind of work, we need to apply force and to apply force, we need energy.

WHAT CAN FORCE DO

Force can stop a moving object.

Force can move an object.

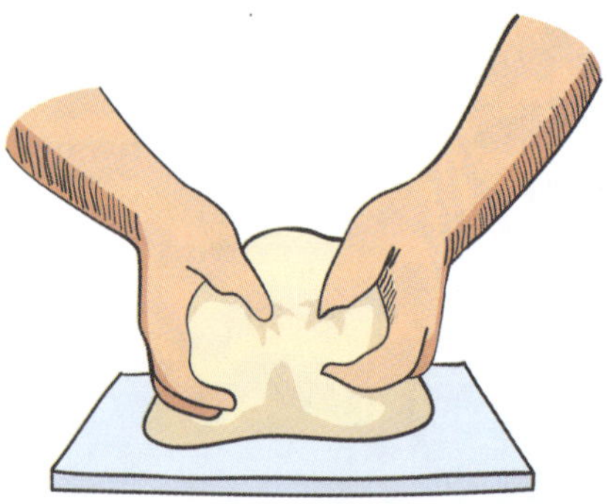

Force can change the shape of an object such as kneading dough.

Force can change the direction and speed of a moving object.

Imagine a cricket match in which a batsman is caught out by the fielder. When the batsman hits the ball with his bat, he moves the ball away from himself by applying force. The fielder who catches the ball also uses force to stop and catch the ball. While the game is going on, the batsman hits the ball in different directions trying to score runs. This explains all the things that force can do. The batsman may hit the ball hard to make it move faster or hit it lightly to make it move slowly.

Your Task

Find out different examples of push and pull that happen in your classroom.

TYPES OF FORCE

Force can be of various types, such as gravitational force or gravity, frictional force, muscular force, mechanical force and magnetic force.

Gravity or gravitational force: Gravity is the force by which the Earth pulls everything towards itself. The force of gravity is acting upon us at all times.

Remember

Sir Isaac Newton was the first person to notice the force of gravity when he observed an apple falling down from a tree.

Your Task

Toss a coin upwards. What happens to it?
It goes up and then comes back down. This shows the effect of gravity.

Friction or frictional force: Friction occurs when two surfaces move or slide against one another. The force of friction opposes (works in opposite direction) the motion of an object, causing the moving object to slow down or to come to a stop completely. If there was no force of friction, a moving object would continue to move and not stop.

Friction between our shoes and the ground prevents us from slipping and the friction between car tyres and the road prevents the car from sliding out of control.

Friction between shoe and the ground

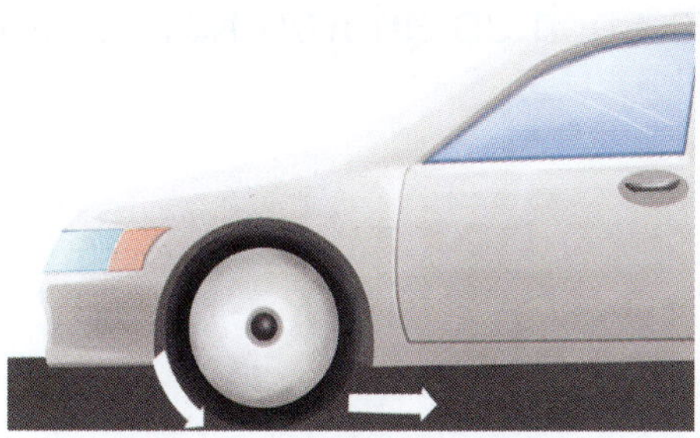

Friction between car tyres and road

Real World

Striking a matchstick against the side of a matchbox gives out spark due to friction between the two surfaces.

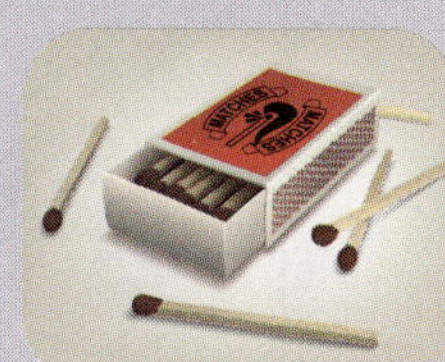

The rougher the surface, the more will be the friction produced. It is easier to pull or push a heavy object over a smooth surface due to less friction.

Friction is reduced by applying **lubricants** to surfaces. You may have seen people applying oil to machine parts in order to make them work smoothly.

My Dictionary

lubricants: substances such as oil and grease which are used for reducing friction

Your Task

Rub your hands together. Do you feel warm? The heat that you feel on your hands is actually a result of friction.

Now, apply some lotion on your palms and spread it evenly. Once again, rub your hands together. Do you still feel the heat?

The lotion will reduce the force of friction and less heat will be produced.

Muscular force: Muscular force is the force applied by your muscles. It is used to pull a chair, lift heavy objects or kick a ball.

Science in Action

Place some heavy books on your desk and push the desk. You are using the muscles of your arms to push the desk.

Real World

A strong person with strong muscles can lift heavier objects than people with weak muscles.

Mechanical force: Sometimes, we use the force of a machine to do things. Such a force is called mechanical force. Pushing bicycle pedals to move forward and using a crane to lift things are examples of mechanical force.

Magnetic force: A magnetic force is caused due to the presence of a magnet. A magnet can pull objects such as an iron key or nail towards it.

A crane lifting weights

Magnet attracting iron nails

Knowledge Check

Fill in the blanks.

1. A force is a ________________ or ________________.
2. When a goalkeeper stops a football from entering a goalpost with his hand, he is using ________________ force.
3. ________________ is a force that pulls everything towards the centre of the Earth.
4. Friction is reduced by applying ________________ to surfaces.
5. A moving football comes to a stop after some time because of the force of ________________.

WORK

In science, work is said to be done when we apply force on an object and it moves in the direction of the force applied or changes position.

Even if we push a wall for a long time with all our might, it will not move. Thus, no work is done. Similarly, when we sit on a chair and study the whole day through, no work is done as we have not moved. However, if we push a chair and move it from one point to another, we would have done some work.

No work done

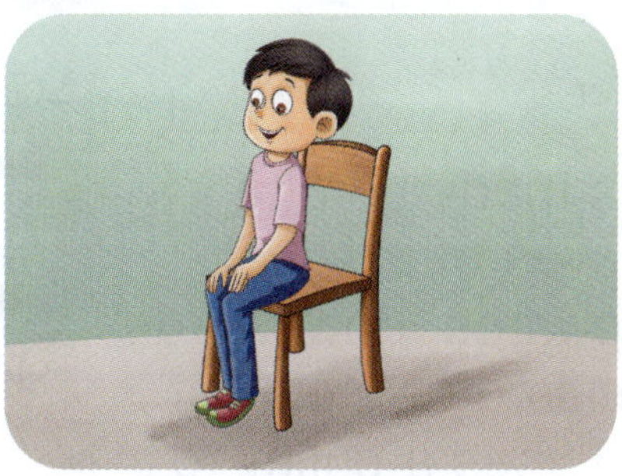
No work done

Work done

SIMPLE MACHINES

In our daily lives, we use different types of machines. These machines make our work easy. They help us to do work with less effort and in less time.

Refrigerator

Washing machine

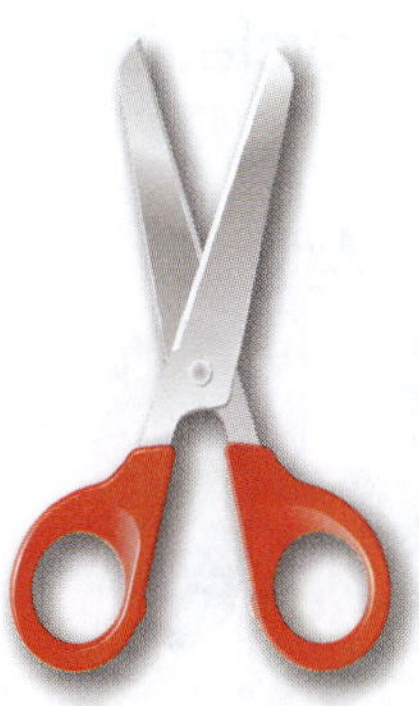
Scissors

Some machines are simple, while some are complex with many parts. Can you name some simple machines that we use every day?

How machines help us

- Machines help us do work easily and with less effort.
- Machines help us do work in less time.
- Machines make our lives easy and comfortable.

The six basic types of machines

Lever: A lever is a simple machine that has two parts: a rod or an arm and a point or a fulcrum around which the lever turns. A lever can help us lift objects, open cans and cut things. Some examples of levers are can opener, nut cracker, scissors, see-saw and hammer.

Lever

Bottle opener

Scissors

Pulley: This simple machine is made up of a rope running between the grooves of a wheel. Pulleys help us move loads upwards, downwards or sideways. Water from a well is drawn out with the help of a pulley. A flagpole uses a pulley to raise or lower a flag. Other examples of pulleys are cranes, blinds and clothes line.

A pulley

Pulley is used to draw water from well.

Wheel and axle: This machine consists of a wheel and a rod known as axle that passes through the centre of the wheel. This allows the wheel to turn and change direction. Moving heavy objects becomes easier with the help of wheel and axle. The wheels of a car and a bicycle, and skates are examples of wheel and axle.

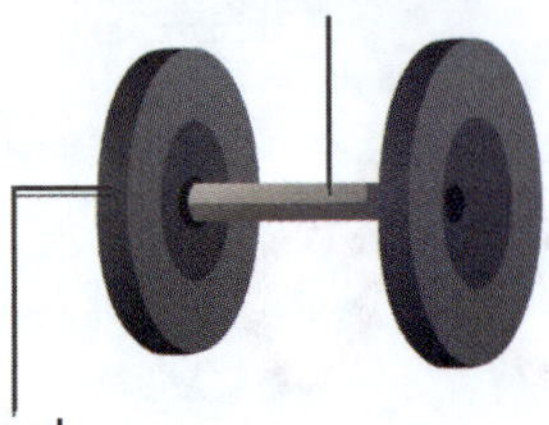

Wheel and axle

Roller skates

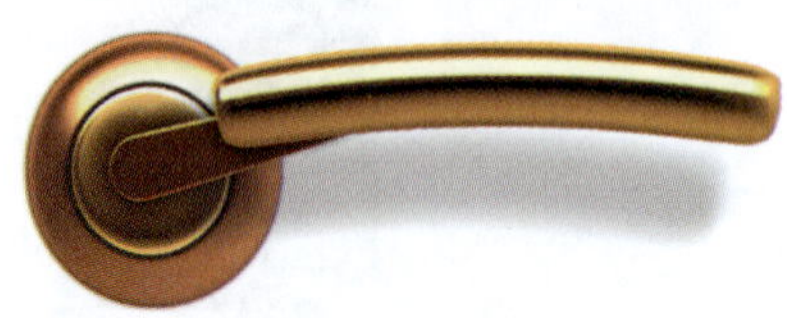

Door knob

Inclined plane: An inclined plane is a flat surface that is higher on one end, that is, it has a slope. It helps to move an object to a lower or higher place thereby making the work of moving things easier. Slides, ramps and escalators are examples of inclined planes.

Ramp

Escalator

Wedge: A wedge is made up of two planes, with one or both inclined or slanting planes, which join together to form a sharp edge. It is used to split things apart. An axe blade, a kitchen knife, a push pin, a nail, a fork and a saw are examples of wedges.

A knife

A push pin

A saw

Screw: A screw consists of an inclined plane wrapped around a cylinder. Screws are used to hold things together. Examples of screws are bolts, bottle caps, bulb caps and key rings.

A bolt

A bottle cap

Cap of a bulb

ENERGY

Energy is the ability to make things work. It can move things (such as a bus) or it can heat up things or produce light.

All living things need energy for life processes. We get energy from the food we eat. This energy is used to work, move and play. Plants use energy from the sun to make food, grow and stay healthy.

Machines also need energy to work. This energy comes from sources such as electricity, wind and fuel.

Energy is all around us. Let us learn about the different sources of energy.

Solar cooker

Sun: The sun is the main source of energy on Earth. The energy from the sun is called the solar energy. All the food that we eat to get energy can be traced back to the sun. Plants do not eat food but use energy from the sun to make food through the process of photosynthesis. We use solar energy to cook food, warm water and light lamps.

Wind: Energy derived from the wind is called wind energy. For example, a windmill uses wind energy to produce electricity.

Water: The energy from water can be used to produce electricity. A dam is a huge wall that is built to block a flowing river, forming a reservoir. Dams use the energy of fast flowing water to produce electricity.

Windmill

Dam

Fossil fuel: Fossils are formed from the remains of dead plants and animals that died millions of years ago. As they lie under the layers of rocks, they slowly change into fossil fuel. We get energy by burning them. Coal, crude oil and natural gas are some examples of fossil fuel. Petrol and diesel are made from crude oil. We burn them to run vehicles. LPG or cooking gas is made from natural gases.

Coal

Some other forms of energy are sound energy, electrical energy, mechanical energy, magnetic energy, heat energy and chemical energy.

Renewable and non-renewable sources of energy

Renewable sources of energy are those that do not get exhausted easily and can be renewed. Wind, water and sun are examples of renewable energy.

Non-renewable sources of energy are those that cannot be renewed easily and will get completely exhausted one day. Petrol, coal and wood are some examples of non-renewable sources.

We should be careful while using non-renewable sources of energy.

Real World

On 14 July 2017, Indian Railways took a green initiative by launching its first solar-powered DEMU train which operates from Delhi to Haryana. A total of 16 solar panels are fitted in its six coaches in order to reduce the fuel consumption.

Your Task

What is the full form of LPG?

LPG cylinder

Concept Map

Force

types

- Gravity
- Friction
- Muscular
- Mechanical
- Magnetic

Simple Machines

types

- Lever
  Example:

  Bottle opener
- Wheel and axle
  Example:

  Door knob
- Pulley
  Example:

  Pulley used in a well to draw water
- Inclined plane
  Example:

  Escalator
- Screw
  Example:

  A bottle cap
- Wedge
  Example:

  A knife

Summary

a. In this chapter, I have learnt that

- Force can change the shape of an object and change the direction and speed of a moving object.
- Work is said to be done when the position of an object changes because of force applied.
- Machines help us work easily with less effort.
- Energy can be renewable or non renewable.

b. I can do the following:

- Talk about the different kinds of force and mention where we see it being applied
- Name the different kinds of simple machines we use in our daily life
- Name the different sources of energy
- Differentiate between renewable and non-renewable energy

Practice ZONE

A. Choose the correct option.

1. ____________ is an example of an inclined plane.
   a. Wheelbarrow b. Ramp c. Screwdriver
2. ____________ is a fossil fuel.
   a. Coal b. Cow dung c. Paper
3. ____________ use the sun's energy.
   a. Microwave ovens b. Solar cookers c. Washing machines
4. ____________ is a renewable source of energy.
   a. Water b. Coal c. Petroleum

B. Write T for true or F for false.

1. Frictional force always works in the opposite direction to motion.
2. A dam uses the energy of cement to produce electricity.
3. The sun is the ultimate source of energy on Earth.
4. A knife is an example of an inclined plane.

C. Fill in the blanks using the words given in the box.

pulley	natural gas	non-renewable	wind

1. Water is drawn from a well with the help of a ________________.
2. A windmill uses ________________ energy to produce electricity.
3. LPG is made from ________________.
4. We should be careful while using ________________ sources of energy.

D. Give two examples for each of these.

1. Applying force
2. Machines that help us in our homes
3. Wedges
4. Screws

E. Give reasons for each of these.

1. A ball rolls faster on a cemented floor than a grassy field.
2. It is easier to move heavy furniture when we put a piece of cardboard under it.

F. Answer these questions in brief.

1. What is force?
2. What is mechanical force? Give an example of mechanical force.
3. Define work.
4. What are the ways in which machines help us?

G. Answer these questions in detail.

1. Write a list of things that force can do.
2. What are the different kinds of machines? Describe briefly and give one example of each.

H. Out of the box!

Most of our cities are polluted by harmful gases in the air. What is responsible for this pollution? How can we make the air cleaner?

I. Picture Talk

What is shown in the picture? What kind of energy does it use? Write any two uses of it.

Skills Enrichment ZONE

A. 21 CS Creativity and Innovation, Technology Literacy | HQ Cooperation and Collaborative Living | AI

With the help of Internet, find out the names and pictures of inventors of five machines. Paste in your scrapbook and present it to your classmates.

B. 21 CS Creativity and Innovation, Life Skills | AI | HQ Knowing My Needs

STEAM Challenge

9 INDUSTRY, INNOVATION AND INFRASTRUCTURE

Invent an unusual machine that could help you to do your school homework. Draw it on a chart paper and describe its functions.

C. 21 CS Critical Thinking, Life Skills

12 RESPONSIBLE CONSUMPTION AND PRODUCTION

Do not waste energy. Put off the lights and fan when you leave a room. Do not waste water; close the tap after use. Walk or use a bicycle to go to places nearby. Write two more ways by which you can save energy.

12 Air, Water and Weather

Prior Knowledge

In the previous classes, I have learnt that

- Air is a mixture of gases.
- Pure water has no colour, smell, taste or shape.
- Both air and water are useful to us.
- Weather changes everyday.

Learning Objectives

In this chapter, I will learn about:

- Weather
- Air
- Sea breeze and land breeze
- Water
- Water cycle
- Water purification

Let's Get Going

Unscramble the weather words.

1. L C I A M E T ____________________
2. E S A S N O ____________________
3. I R D E Z L Z ____________________
4. L C U O D Y ____________________

WEATHER

Weather is the condition of the atmosphere of a place at a particular time. It is not same everywhere. Weather changes from hour to hour and day to day. It may be sunny in the morning but cloudy in the evening. It may be foggy one day and rainy the next day. Weather also changes from season to season. It is hot in summer but cold in winter.

What causes changes in weather?

The sun affects the weather. It heats up the land, air and water to bring about a change in the weather. Other factors like wind, air, clouds and rain also cause a change in weather.

Real World

- Climate is the average weather of a particular place at different times of the year. When weather remains the same over a long period of time, we call it season.
- The movement of the Earth around the sun is called revolution. The Earth takes 365 days and 6 hours to complete one revolution.

The revolution of the Earth around the sun causes seasons. The Earth is tilted on its axis. As it revolves around the sun in its orbit, the part of the Earth that faces the sun has longer and warmer days, resulting in summer. The part of the Earth that is away from the sun has shorter and cooler days, causing winter.

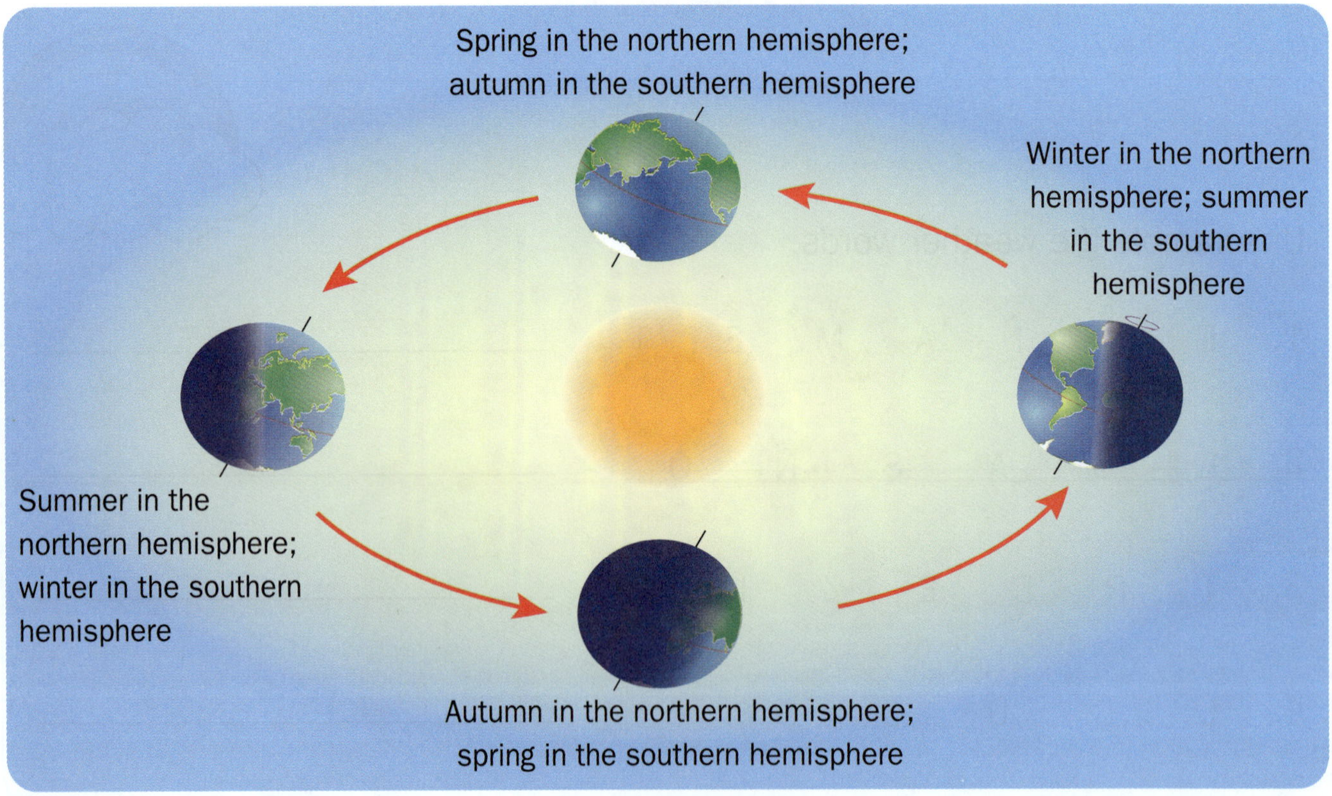

Formation of seasons

We have three main seasons in India: summer, monsoon and winter. In some parts of India, we also have spring and autumn.

AIR

Air is all around us. We cannot see it but can feel it. Air is a mixture of gases. It contains nitrogen, oxygen, water vapour, dust and smoke particles and other gases such as carbon dioxide and argon. The blanket of air around us is called **atmosphere**.

How does wind blow?

You have already learned that moving air is called wind. A gentle wind is called a **breeze** and a very fast and strong wind is called a **storm**. Wind blows due to the heat of the sun. When the air gets heated up, it becomes lighter and therefore rises above the ground. The cool air, that is heavier, then takes up the space left by the hot air. This continuous movement of air causes winds.

Sea breeze and land breeze

We feel the breeze in coastal areas or in areas that are next to water bodies. This is because water takes longer to heat up and can retain heat for a longer time.

Sea breeze

During the day, the land gets heated up quickly and the air above the land warms up faster than the air above the sea. As the warm air rises, the cool wind blows towards the land to occupy the space created by it. This cool air is called sea breeze. It blows in the daytime.

Formation of sea breeze

Your Task

Take a cup of water and keep it outside on a hot summer day. After an hour, feel the water in the cup and touch the land around. Which one is hotter? This shows that land gets hot faster than water.

Land breeze

At night, the land quickly loses its heat, while the sea retains its warmth. This means the air over the water is warmer and lighter and therefore begins to rise. The cool wind above the land begins to move towards the sea to replace the rising warm air. This cool air that blows from the land is called land breeze. It blows only at night.

Formation of land breeze

WATER

Water is very important for life on Earth. We need water for various purposes in our daily lives. Plants and animals also need water to survive. Ice, water and water vapour are the three forms of water.

Evaporation

Have you ever wondered what happens to the water present in wet clothes when you dry them in the sunlight? Where does water in the puddles formed after a heavy shower go?

The heat of the sun changes water into water vapour that merges with the air around. The process of water changing into water vapour on being heated is called evaporation. Evaporation takes place everywhere and at all times.

The amount of water vapour present in the air is called **humidity**. During hot weather, more water gets evaporated and makes the weather humid.

Factors that affect evaporation

There are some factors that affect the rate of evaporation. These include:

- **Temperature:** The higher is the temperature, the faster is the evaporation.
- **Wind:** Wind helps water to evaporate faster. The stronger is the wind, the higher is the rate of evaporation.
- **Humidity:** Lesser water vapour or humidity results in drier air, leading to a higher rate of evaporation. Thus, clothes dry faster in summer than in the rainy season.
- **Surface area:** The greater is the exposed surface area, the higher is the rate of evaporation. This is why we spread out the clothes for drying rather than keeping the wet clothes in a pile.

Your Task

- Take two cups filled with an equal amount of water. Keep one cup in the garden and other in the classroom. Observe the water in both the cups.
- You will see the water kept outside will evaporate faster than the water kept in the classroom. Why?
- Take equal amount of water in a glass and a flat dish and place it in the sun. Which one evaporates faster? Why?

Condensation

Just as the state of water changes on heating, its state also changes on cooling or by losing heat.

Take a bottle of cold water from the fridge and keep it outside on a table. You will see droplets of water forming on the outer surface of the bottle. This happens as the air around the bottle, on coming in contact with the bottle, cools down and changes into water vapour.

The process by which a gas changes into liquid on cooling is called condensation.

Droplets of water formed on the surface of bottle due to condensation

Tiny drops of water on leaves formed by condensation of water vapour present in air

What happens when you fill up an ice-tray with water and put it in the freezer? After a while, you see that the water has changed into ice. The process in which a liquid becomes a solid is called **freezing**. When solid turns into liquid, it is called **melting**.

Freezing

Melting

WATER CYCLE

> **Remember**
>
> Hail, snow, sleet, rain and dew are different forms of precipitation.

The heat of the sun changes water found in water bodies (lakes, rivers, oceans, ponds, etc.) into water vapour (**evaporation**). As the water vapour rises, it comes in contact with the cold air and cools down (**condensation**). The water vapour then changes into tiny drops of water and forms clouds. When the drops become too heavy and the clouds can no longer hold them, they fall to the ground as rain, hail or snow. This is called **precipitation**. This process where water is constantly moving in a cycle from the surface of the Earth to the sky and then back to the ground is called the **water cycle**. This cycle goes on all the time in the nature.

Some of the water that falls down seeps into the ground and is stored as **underground water**. We dig wells or use tubewells to pump out this water.

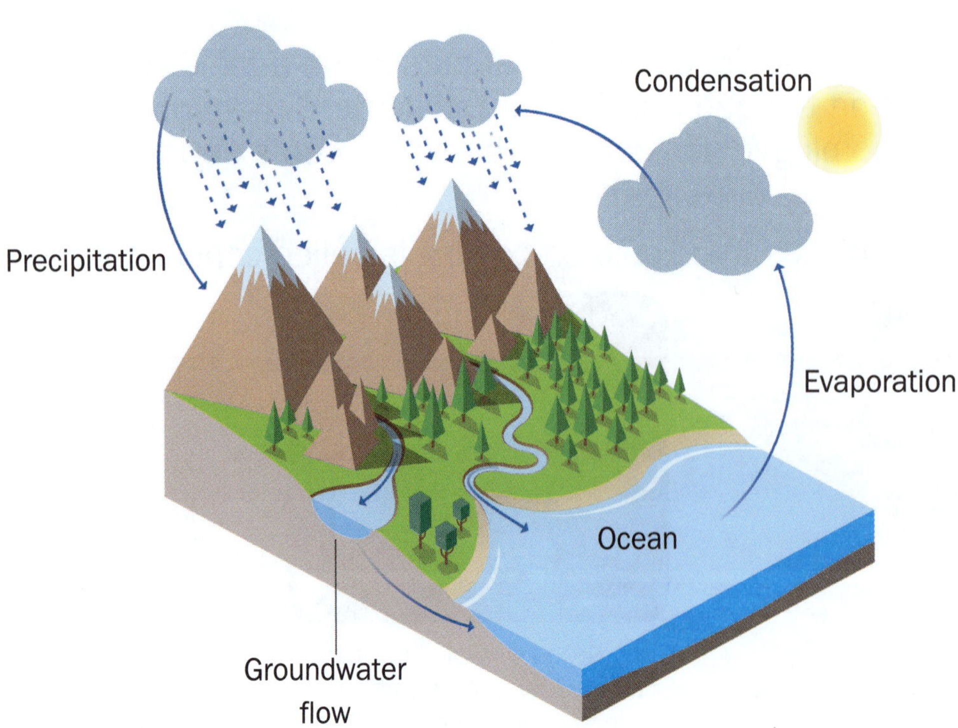

Water cycle

> **Talk About**
>
> What would happen if there was no water cycle in nature?

Knowledge Check

Fill in the blanks.

1. The blanket of air around us is called ______________.
2. The heat of ______________ causes winds to blow.
3. The amount of water vapour present in air is called ______________.
4. The process of changing water into ice is called ______________.
5. The higher is the temperature, the ______________ is the evaporation.

WATER PURIFICATION

Sometimes, water looks clear but it may contain germs and other impurities.

Impurities that dissolve in water and are not visible to the naked eye are called **soluble impurities**. Impurities that are not soluble in water and can be easily seen are called **insoluble impurities**.

To keep ourselves healthy, we must drink water that has been purified. Impure water may cause diseases such as cholera, diarrhoea and typhoid.

Ways to remove insoluble impurities present in water

Sedimentation and decantation: In this method, water is kept undisturbed for some time. The heavy impurities settle down at the bottom of the container, leaving the clear water on top. This process is called sedimentation.

The clear water on top is slowly poured into another container. This is called decantation.

Filtration: Filtration is a process by which insoluble impurities are separated by passing the water through filters. Usually a filter paper is folded in the shape of a cone and fitted in a funnel through which the water is passed. It holds back the solid impurities and allows the clean water to pass.

Sedimentation Decantation Filtration

Talk About

We cannot drink sea water directly. Why?

Ways to remove soluble impurities

Boiling: The easiest way to purify water is to boil it for 10 to 15 minutes. It kills all the germs.

Boiling

Chlorination: Chlorination is a process in which chlorine gas or chlorine tablets are added to kill germs and make the water fit for drinking.

Water is very valuable for the lives of all living things. We need water for carrying out daily activities such as cooking, bathing, drinking etc. It is precious and scarce, and we must never waste it.

Real World

In many homes, drinking water is purified by RO machines. Though we get pure drinking water through this process, a lot of water is wasted.

Talk About

How is water purified for drinking in your home?

Knowledge Check

State T for true or F for false.

1. Sedimentation is used to separate soluble impurities dissolved in water.
2. In filtration, insoluble impurities are separated from water by passing it through filters.
3. Boiling water for 10 to 15 minutes, kills germs.
4. In chlorination method, the heavy impurities present in water settle down at the bottom of the container.
5. We have abundant water in oceans and seas, so, there is no need to save it.

Concept Map

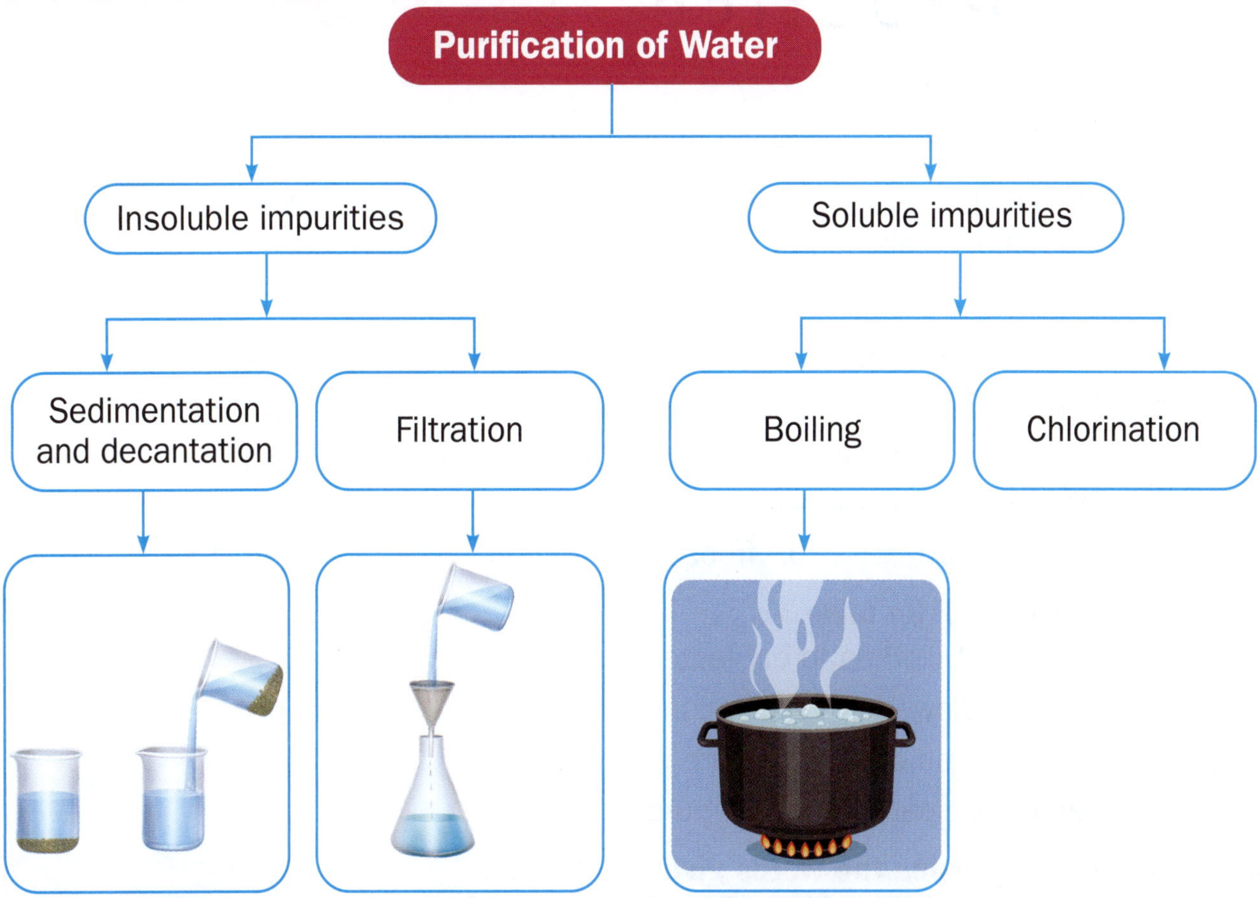

Summary

a. In this chapter, I have learnt that

- Weather is the condition of the atmosphere of a place at a particular time.
- The factors that cause changes in the weather are the sun, wind, air, clouds and rain.
- The blanket of air around us is called the atmosphere.
- Sea breeze blows in the day while land breeze blows at night.
- The factors that affect evaporation are temperature, wind, humidity and surface area.
- Purification of soluble and insoluble impurities in water can be done through sedimentation and decantation, filtration, boiling and chlorination.

b. I can do the following:

- Explain what causes changes in weather
- Talk about the effect of land breeze and sea breeze
- Describe water cycle
- Differentiate between soluble and insoluble impurities in water
- Demonstrate the different processes of purification of water

Practice ZONE

A. Choose the correct option.

1. We use a ____________ to get underground water.

   a. handpump b. tap c. bucket

2. We can remove soluble impurities in water by ____________.

   a. filtration b. boiling c. decantation

3. ____________ is a special paper that traps insoluble impurities.

   a. Blotting paper b. Butter paper c. Filter paper

4. Water droplets forming on the outside of a glass containing cold water is an example of ____________.

   a. condensation b. freezing c. watering

B. Write T for true or F for false.

1. We spread out clothes to dry faster.
2. Land breeze blows from sea to land.
3. We may fall ill on drinking impure water.
4. If water looks clear, it must be pure.

C. Fill in the blanks using the words given in the box.

revolution	insoluble	faster	daytime	night

1. Sea breeze is formed during the ____________ and land breeze is formed at ____________.
2. The ____________ of the Earth causes seasons.
3. The process of sedimentation is used to purify water from ____________ impurities.
4. Water evaporates ____________ when the temperature is higher.

D. Give reasons for each of these.

1. Some people boil water for drinking.
2. We sweat a lot on a hot day during the monsoon.
3. Coastal areas are cooler during the day.

E. Answer these questions in brief.

1. What is weather? What are the factors that control weather?
2. How is evaporation affected by humidity and wind?
3. How can we remove soluble impurities from water?
4. What are the different components of air?

F. Answer these questions in detail.

1. What are land breeze and sea breeze? How are they formed?
2. What is water cycle? Explain the cycle of water in nature.
3. With diagrams explain the two ways in which we can remove insoluble impurities from water.

G. Out of the box!

After floods, the government often distributes chlorine tablets to the affected people. Why?

H. Picture Talk

1. Label the water cycle.

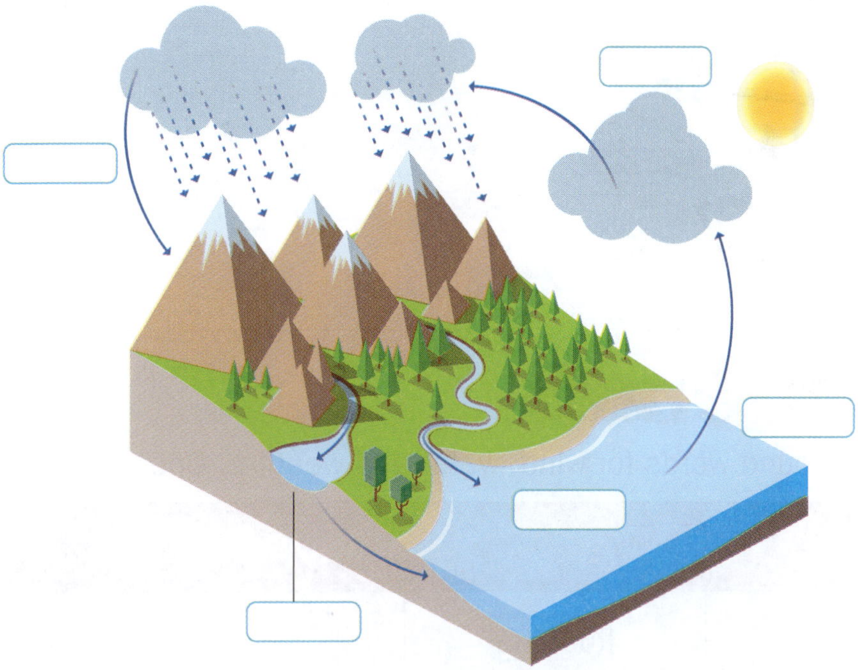

2. Identify the movement of the wind. Talk about the effects of such winds.

Skills Enrichment ZONE

A. 21 CS Information Literacy

9 INDUSTRY, INNOVATION AND INFRASTRUCTURE

Given below are the pictures of some instruments that provide us information about different factors of weather. Find out the names of these weather instruments and their uses.

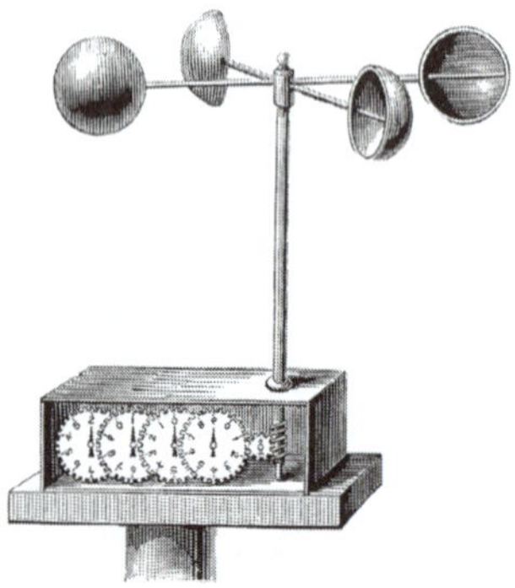

________________ ________________ ________________

B. 21 CS Critical Thinking CC Integration with English

Give action/sound words for wind, water and weather. One has been done for you.

	Action/Sound words		
Wind	Rustling		
Water	Flowing		
Weather	Thundering		

C. 21 CS Critical Thinking; Creativity and Innovation HQ Coexisting with Nature AI CC Integration with English

12 RESPONSIBLE CONSUMPTION AND PRODUCTION

Rohan's mother collects the leftover water from the used water bottles or buckets to water the plants. Do you also do anything like this to save water? Write a short note on it. Also, make a small poster to motivate people about saving water.

Worksheet 4

STEAM CHALLENGE

Ali, a student of Class 4, visited his grandparents who live in a village. He was surprised to see that the lifestyle of the people in the village was very different from the people living in a city. Grandfather told Ali many things about how people in olden days used to live when there was no electricity. Grandfather also told him that there were no water purifiers in olden days. Ali asked his grandfather about how people in olden days used to purify water.

Help Ali to make a model of the water purifier used by people in those days.

What is the challenge?

What supplies do you need?

1

2

What worked or did not work for you?

How can you improve it?

Hydrologic Cycle

The Hydrologic Cycle/Water Cycle is the continuous circulation of water from Earth to the atmosphere and back again.

Forests are a critical part of the cycle. They contribute to rainfall and groundwater. Rain clouds are formed when water evaporates. Trees also contribute to the formation of rainclouds through transpiration: release of water vapour through leaves.

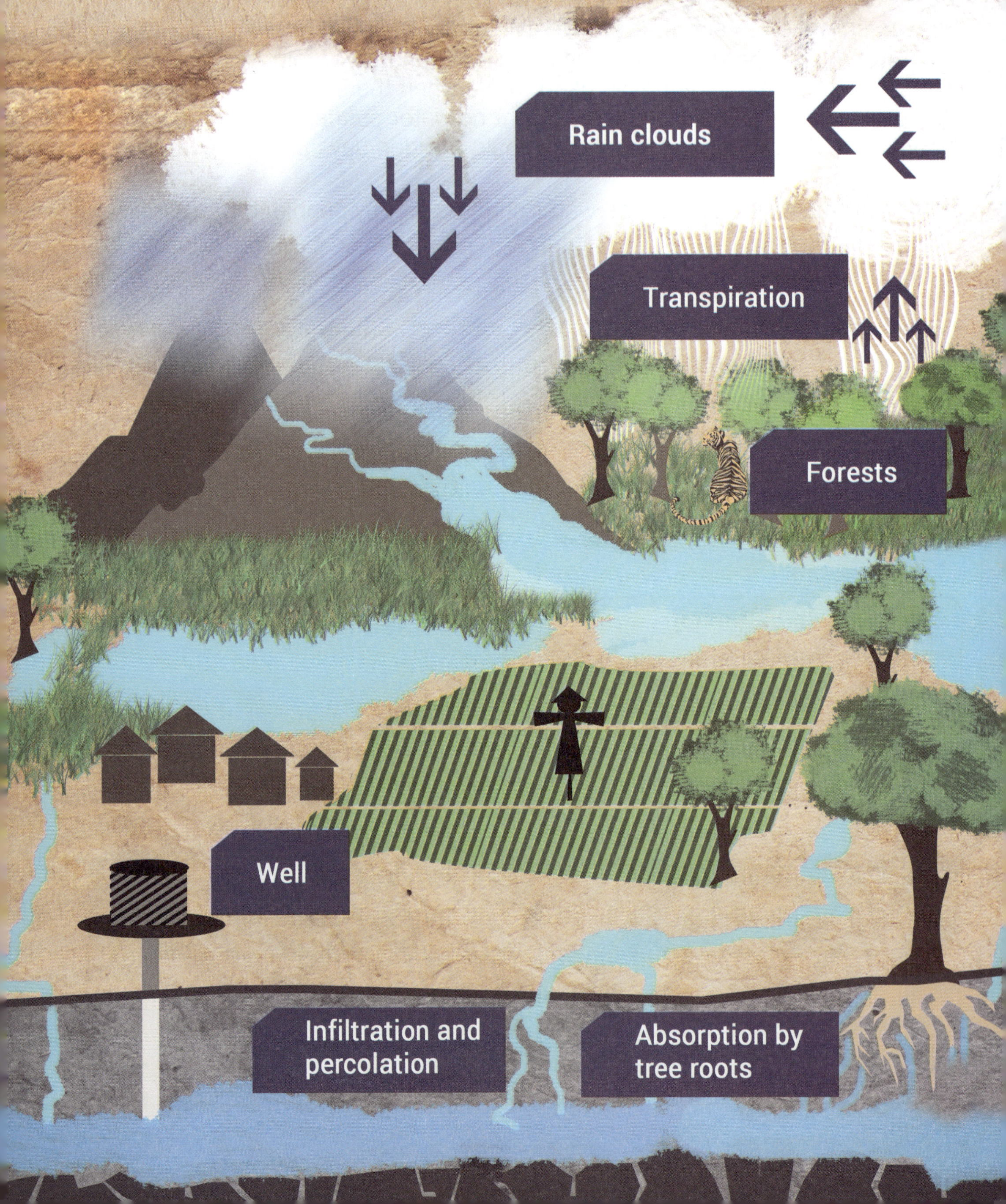

When it rains, some of the water percolates into the soil. Natural healthy forests have deep root systems that absorb and store this water and help recharge the water table.
Tree roots draw up groundwater into the trees, and plants again. More than 100 rivers originate in the tiger forests of the Satpuda range.
Over 2 crore (20 million) people depend on them for water!

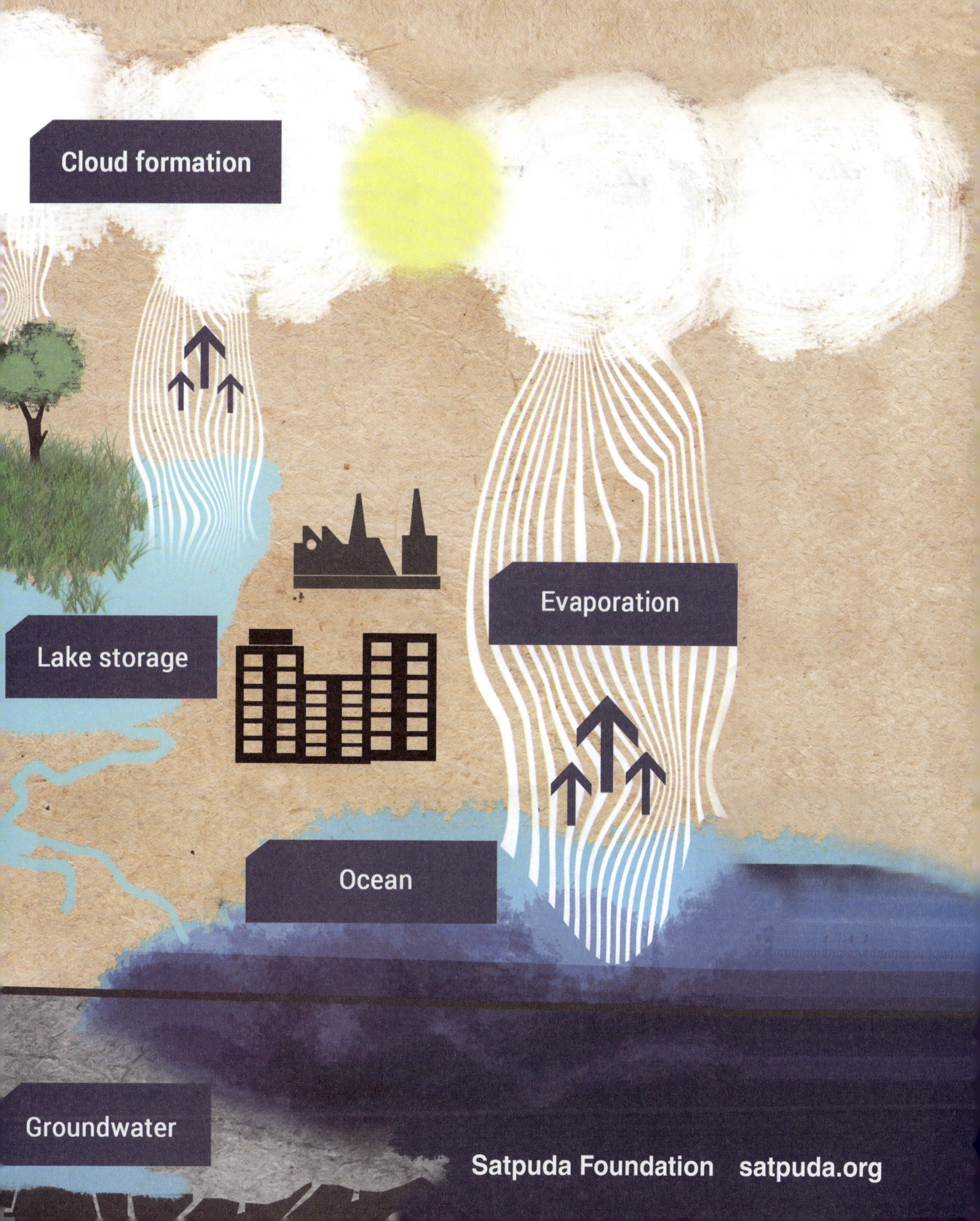

Satpuda Foundation satpuda.org

13 Our Universe

Prior Knowledge

In the previous classes, I have learnt that

- Earth is a living planet.
- Sun and the eight planets revolving around it make our solar system.
- Moon is the natural satellite of the Earth.

Learning Objectives

In this chapter, I will learn about:

- Stars
- Planets
- Satellites
- Solar system
- Movements of the Earth

Let's Get Going

Can you name these planets?

What do you see when you look up at the sky? You see the sun, moon and stars. All these are heavenly bodies that exist in space. Space is the place beyond the Earth's atmosphere.

The term universe means everything that exists. The stars, the sun, the moon, the planets, the galaxies and everything found in space make up the universe. The Earth and all the living and non-living things are part of this universe.

STARS

Stars are huge balls of gases found in space. They continuously give out heat and light. The stars are stationary and do not change their position. There are thousands of stars in the universe. They are very big in size. They look small as they are very far from us. The sun is also a star. It looks big as it is the closest to the Earth.

Stars in the night sky

Remember

- The stars do not actually twinkle. They seem to twinkle because of the movement of air in the Earth's atmosphere.
- The light from stars takes millions of years to reach the Earth; therefore, when we look at the stars we are actually looking back in time.

PLANETS

Planets are heavenly bodies that revolve around the sun in their fixed elliptical (oval) paths. These paths are called orbits. Unlike stars, planets do not have light of their own. They shine due to the light of the sun.

Your Task

What is Mangalyaan?

SATELLITES

A satellite is a heavenly body that moves around a planet in an orbit. Moon is the natural satellite of the Earth. The other planets also have moons. Mercury and Venus are the only planets that do not have any moon.

Moon orbiting the Earth

Real World

- Man-made satellites sent to space help in weather forecasting, broadcasting radio and television programmes and distant communication.
- Moon is the only heavenly body other than the Earth on which humans have set foot.

SOLAR SYSTEM

You have learnt in Class 3 that the sun and its family of eight planets form the solar system.
The solar system also contains comets, moons, dwarf planets, dust and gases.

The planets in order of their distance from the sun are Mercury, Venus, Earth, Mars, Jupiter, Saturn, Uranus and Neptune. Let us learn more about each member of the solar system.

Your Task

What are sunspots?

Real World

A comet is a small chunk of dust and ice that orbits or travels around the sun. It is sometimes called as a dirty snowball.

Solar system (not to scale)

Sun

The sun is at the centre of the solar system. Like other stars, it is a huge ball of hot gases. It gives us heat and light.

Sun

Mercury

Mercury is the smallest planet in the solar system and the closest to the sun. Mercury takes only 88 days to revolve around the sun.

Mercury

Venus

Venus is the second planet from the sun. Being the brightest planet, it can be easily spotted in the sky and is also known as the 'evening star'. Though it is not the closest planet to the sun, it is the hottest planet in the solar system.

Venus

Earth

Earth

Earth is the third planet from the sun. It is the only planet that has conditions suitable to sustain life and is, therefore, known as the 'living planet'. Living things can survive on Earth because it has water, air and a favourable temperature. Earth is also known as the 'blue planet' because seventy per cent of its surface is made up of water. Hence, when seen from space, it appears blue.

Mars

Mars

Mars is the fourth planet from the sun. It is also known as the 'red planet' because it is full of red-coloured dust and rocks.

Jupiter

Jupiter

Jupiter is the fifth planet from the sun and the largest planet in the solar system. It is so big that it can fit in more than 1000 Earths within itself. Despite the big size, it spins very fast on its axis. This fast spinning causes storms on Jupiter. The planet has the maximum number of moons (over 60) going around it.

Saturn

Saturn

Saturn is the sixth planet from the sun and the second largest in the solar system. It is considered to be the most beautiful planet due to the spectacular system of rings around it.

Uranus

Uranus

Uranus is the seventh planet from the sun. It cannot be seen from the Earth without a telescope. It is the third largest planet in the solar system and has 27 moons.

Neptune

Neptune

Neptune is the eighth planet and the farthest from the sun. It experiences the most violent weather in the solar system. It has 14 known moons.

The planets in the solar system belong to two groups. The **inner planets** consist of Mercury, Venus, Earth and Mars. And the **outer planets** consist of Jupiter, Saturn, Uranus and Neptune.

The inner planets are made of rocks and are thus called the **rocky planets**.

The outer planets are made of frozen gases and called the **gas giants**.

The outer and the inner planets are separated by an **asteroid belt**. An asteroid belt is a ring made of rocks and metals that orbit the sun.

Pluto

Pluto, which was considered to be a planet earlier, is now known as a dwarf planet due to its small size.

Knowledge Check

Underline the incorrect words in the sentences and write the correct ones in the blanks.

1. Mercury is the hottest planet. ____________
2. Saturn is the largest planet. ____________
3. A satellite is a heavenly body that goes around the sun. ____________
4. Uranus is a rocky planet. ____________

MOVEMENTS OF THE EARTH

The Earth shows two types of movements: rotation and revolution.

Your Task

Why we cannot go on a holiday to other planets?

Rotation

The movement of the Earth on its own axis is called rotation. The axis is an imaginary vertical line that passes through the centre of the Earth, running from the North Pole to the South Pole. The Earth takes 24 hours to complete one rotation. The rotation of the Earth causes day and night. As the Earth rotates, the half that faces the sun has day, while the other half that is away from the sun has night. The Earth rotates from west to east.

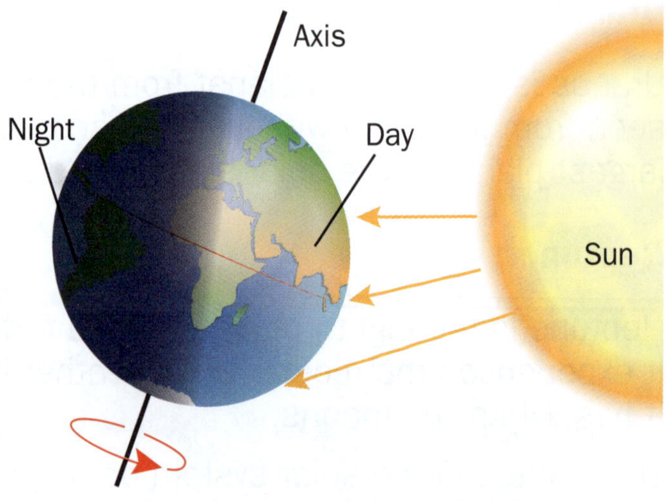

Rotation causes day and night

Real World

An imaginary line around the middle of the Earth (at an equal distance from the North Pole and the South Pole) dividing the Earth into two hemispheres–northern and southern—is called the equator.

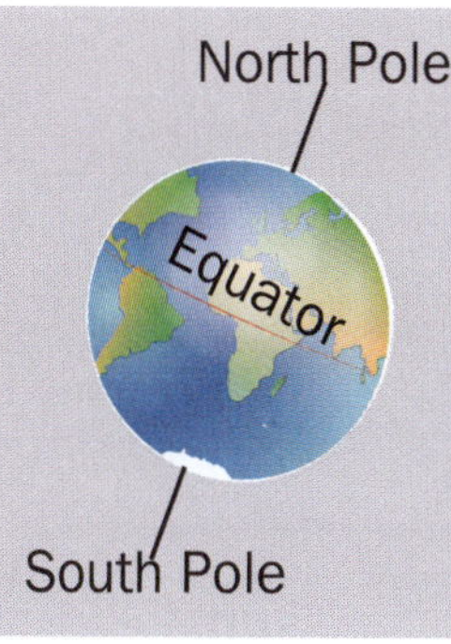

Let's Try

Darken the classroom and switch off the fans. Light a candle and imagine it to be the sun. Take a small paper cutout of a human figure and consider it to be you. Find your location on a globe and stick the figure over there. Place the globe in front of the candle. You will see that the side of the globe (with you on that side) that faces the candle lights up. So, you are now directly facing the sunlight and it is day time for you. The other side of the globe does not receive any sunlight and is dark. So, it is night time on the other side.

Now, slowly rotate the globe. You will see that the dark side of the globe is now facing the sunlight, while your side is now in darkness. This explains how rotation causes day and night.

REVOLUTION

The movement of the Earth around the sun in its fixed elliptical orbit is called revolution.

The Earth takes $365\frac{1}{4}$ days to revolve around the sun.

This is equal to one year on Earth.

Talk About

Which is your favourite season and why?

In the previous chapter, we learnt that revolution causes seasons. When Earth revolves around the sun on its tilted axis, one half of the Earth is nearer to the sun, while the other half is away from it. The half nearer to the sun receives direct sunlight and has hotter and longer days. Thus, it has summer.

At the same time, the other half of the Earth that is away from the sun receives slanted sunlight and hence the days are shorter and cooler here. This half of the Earth has winter.

In between these two seasons, the Earth experiences autumn and spring, which are neither too hot nor too cold.

Your Task

Place a candle at the centre of a room. Hold a globe in your hand and walk around the candle to show revolution of the Earth. At the same time, spin the globe slowly to show rotation.

Concept Map

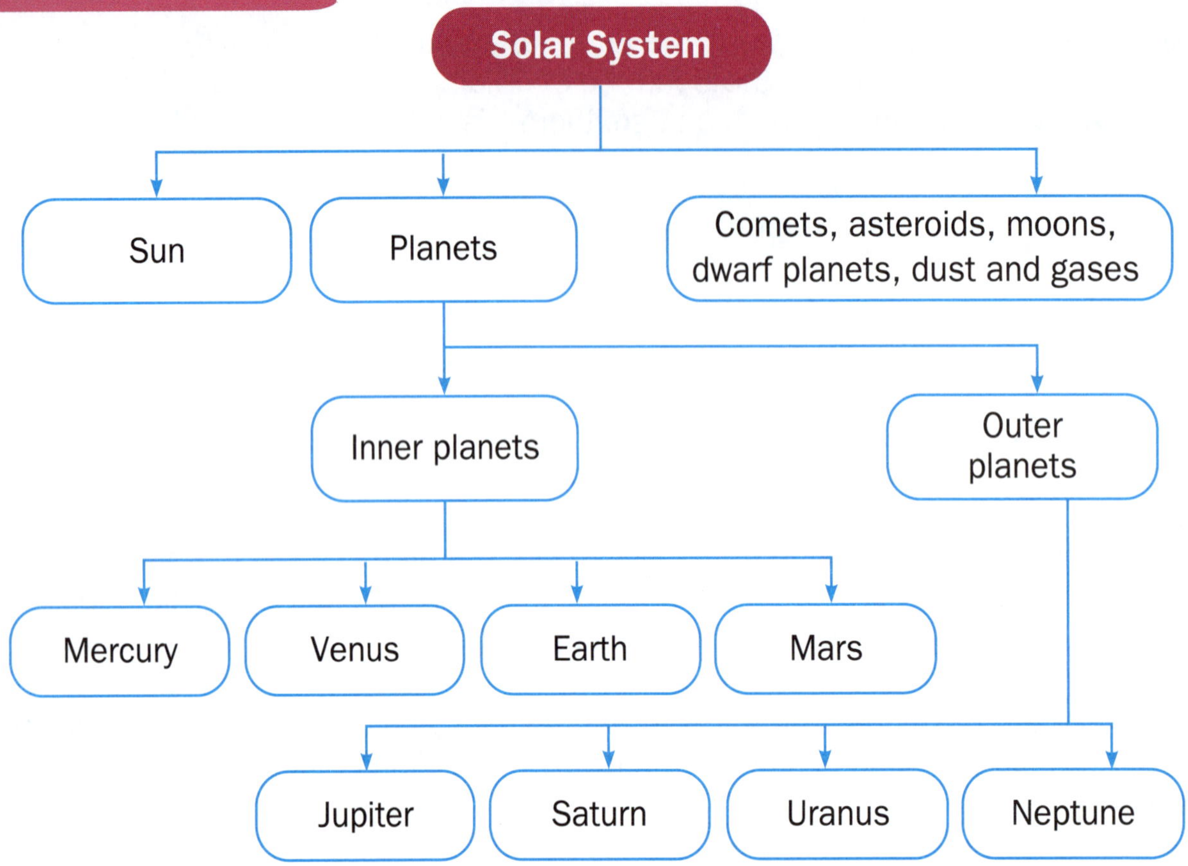

Summary

a. In this chapter, I have learnt that

- Stars are huge balls of gases found in space.
- Planets are heavenly bodies that revolve around the sun in their fixed elliptical paths called orbits.
- A satellite is a heavenly body that moves around a planet.
- The Earth shows two types of movements, that is, rotation and revolution.
- The rotation of the Earth causes day and night and the revolution of the Earth causes seasons.

b. I can do the following:

- Name all the planets of the solar system and describe them
- Understand and explain how rotation causes day and night
- Explain how revolution causes seasons
- Label the solar system

Practice ZONE

A. Choose the correct option.

1. ____________ does not have satellites.
   a. Uranus   b. Jupiter   c. Mercury
2. ____________ is called the 'evening star'.
   a. Venus   b. Mars   c. Mercury
3. ____________ has the largest number of satellites.
   a. Uranus   b. Jupiter   c. Neptune
4. ____________ is the nearest to the sun.
   a. Earth   b. Mercury   c. Venus

B. Write T for true or F for false.

1. The outer planets are made up of frozen gas.
2. The path followed by planets is circular.
3. Pluto is a dwarf planet.
4. The revolution of the Earth causes day and night.

C. Fill in the blanks using the words given in the box.

Mars	rocky	Mercury	Jupiter	orbit

1. The inner planets are also called ____________ planets.
2. The path followed by a planet is called its ____________.
3. ____________ is also called the 'red planet'.
4. ____________ is the smallest and ____________ is the largest planet of our solar system.

D. Give reasons for each of these.

1. Pluto is called a dwarf planet.
2. We cannot see moon during the day.
3. No planet except the Earth has life.

E. Answer these questions in brief.

1. Why is the Earth called the 'blue planet'?
2. What do you mean by 'universe'?
3. What is the asteroid belt and where does it lie?
4. How does the Earth have day and night?

F. Answer these questions in detail.

1. Name all the components of the solar system. Name the eight planets in order of their increasing distance from the sun.
2. How are seasons caused?

G. Out of the box!

All vehicles need fuel. How can the spacecrafts that are sent to Mars and beyond able to fly for years?

H. Picture Talk

What does this picture show?

Skills Enrichment ZONE

A. 21 CS Creativity and Innovation, Collaboration | AI

In groups, make a model of the solar system using plastic balls of different sizes and a cut out of the sun. Stick them on a chart paper and label them in order. You may add some facts about the planets too!

B. 21 CS Information Literacy | HQ Coexisting with Nature

9 INDUSTRY, INNOVATION AND INFRASTRUCTURE

Energy from the sun (solar energy) can be used to light solar bulbs. Use these bulbs and save electricity and money. Can you name some other instruments that work on solar energy?

C. 21 CS Critical Thinking, | CC Integration with English

Imagine that you are a Martian from Mars who has come to Earth. Write five things that you like about the planet Earth and five things that you do not like about it.

14 Our Green Earth

Prior Knowledge

In the previous classes, I have learnt that

- Earth is the only planet in our solar system that has life.
- Pollution of land, air and water has posed many problems for living organisms.
- It is our responsibility to take care of the Earth.

Learning Objectives

In this chapter, I will learn about:

- Importance of trees
- Deforestation
- Keeping the Earth green

Let's Get Going

Look at the picture. Why do you think the child is wearing a mask? Write in the space given below.

____

____

____

____

____

Air in the cities contains a lot of impurities. Dirty air is making it difficult for living things to breathe. If we do not do anything to keep the air clean, we will all be sick and unfit.

Plants clean the air by giving us oxygen. They make our surroundings look green and beautiful. However, to meet the needs of increasing population of human beings, we have destroyed forests by cutting down the trees.

Your Task

Find out the name of a tree, leaves of which are used to cure skin diseases.

IMPORTANCE OF TREES

Trees are of great use to us. They give us many things that we need in our daily lives. Here are some of the important uses of trees.

Forest

- They give us fruits, vegetables, flowers, leaves, stems, spices and seeds as food.
- They purify air by absorbing carbon dioxide and giving out oxygen.
- They are used to make medicines.
- They help in the formation of rain.
- They are home to many animals, especially birds and insects.
- They keep our surroundings cool.
- The roots of trees hold the soil and prevent soil erosion.
- They give us wood for making paper, furniture, doors and windows.
- They give us forest products like resins, gum and rubber.
- Firewood from trees is used as fuel.

Wooden table

Firewood

Real World

- Quinine, used for making medicine for malaria, is made from the bark of cinchona trees.
- Rubber is made from the sap of the rubber tree. The sap is called latex.
- We get resin, which is a sap, from trees. It is used for making varnish and polish.

DEFORESTATION

Destroying forests by cutting down trees in large numbers is called deforestation.

Deforestation

- Deforestation destroys the homes of animals (habitat). It is because of deforestation that we often hear of tigers, elephants and monkeys coming into villages and towns in search of food.
- Cutting down trees has harmful effects on our environment as it reduces rainfall.
- Soil erosion occurs when we cut down too many trees.
- Air becomes unclean as no fresh oxygen is being added by the trees.

Knowledge Check

Fill in the blanks.

1. Plants ________________ the air.
2. Roots hold onto the soil and stop ________________.
3. Cutting down of trees in large numbers is called ________________.
4. Firewood from trees is used as ________________.

KEEPING THE EARTH GREEN

To control the harmful effects of deforestation, we need to plant more trees than we have cut down.

Here are some of the ways to save trees and keep our Earth green.

- We should not waste things made from wood, such as paper. We should use them wisely.
- We should try to reuse things made from trees.
- We should not use wood from trees as firewood for cooking, grilling and roasting.
- We should take steps to control and prevent forest fires.
- We should plant more trees. Planting trees in large numbers is called afforestation.

Save trees, save Earth!

Cutting down trees without permission is a crime. We must not do it and report such acts to the government.

World Environment Day is celebrated on 5th June every year to remind us that we must look after our environment. People all over the world are encouraged to plant more trees.

Children planting a tree

Real World

Trees in the forest sometimes catch fire due to natural causes or by the carelessness of humans. Forest fires burn down trees and kill forest animals.

Van Mahotsava is a tree planting festival, celebrated every year in July in India. During this festival, people plant trees or saplings (baby plants) in their homes, schools, colleges, offices, etc.

On 22nd April, we celebrate the **Earth Day** to remind ourselves that we must take care of the Earth.

Remember

In 1928, Rabindranath Tagore started the *Vriksharopana Utsav* (tree planting ceremony) by planting a sapling in Shantiniketan. The ceremony continues till date.

Earth Day

Act Green

Reuse your old T-shirts to make shopping bags with the help of your parents.

Concept Map

- **Importance of Trees**
  - Provide food
  - Give oxygen
  - Help in rainfall
  - Prevent soil erosion
  - Provide medicines and many other products such as rubber, gum and resins
  - Provide wood for furniture and firewood

- **Important Environmental Events**
  - World Environment Day on 5th June
  - Earth Day on 22nd April
  - Van Mahotsava in July

Summary

a. In this chapter, I have learnt that

- Trees are very important to us.
- Destroying forests by cutting down trees in large numbers is called deforestation and it has harmful effects on all living beings and the environment.
- We should plant more trees.
- 5th June is celebrated as the World Environment Day.
- We must keep the Earth clean.
- 22nd April is celebrated as the Earth Day.

b. I can do the following:

- Talk about the usefulness of trees and the importance of planting trees
- Not waste things made from trees
- Reuse things made from trees

Practice ZONE

A. Choose the correct option.

1. ____________ is a forest product.

   a. Resin b. Leather c. Wool

2. ____________ is a harmful effect of deforestation.

   a. Increase of population

   b. Adulteration in food

   c. Less rainfall

3. Earth Day is celebrated on ____________ every year.

   a. 25th December b. 22nd April c. 26th January

B. Write T for true or F for false.

1. Trees help in the formation of rain.
2. We can make the Earth a cleaner place by cutting down all the trees.
3. Van Mahotsava is a tree planting festival.

C. Fill in the blanks using the words given in the box.

5th June	fire	afforestation

1. Lighting matches in the forest may cause a ____________.
2. Planting trees in large numbers is called ____________.
3. World Environment Day is celebrated on ____________ every year.

D. Give reasons for each of these.

1. Trees save the environment.
2. Increase in population is harmful.
3. In the past few years, the population of monkeys has increased in cities.

E. Answer these questions in brief.

1. What is deforestation? State any two effects of deforestation.
2. Why should one be careful with fire in forests?
3. What days are celebrated to remind people of the importance of plants?

F. Answer these questions in detail.

1. Write five ways in which plants are important to life on Earth.
2. Write down four ways in which we can make our Earth green.

G. Out of the box!

If tree was a person, what qualities would you attribute to it?

H. Picture Talk

1. Why do you think the child is hugging the tree?

2. Write a slogan for your poster to spread awareness about the importance of the World Environment Day.

___

___

___

Skills Enrichment ZONE

A. 21 CS Creativity and Innovation, Collaboration | HQ Coexisting with Nature | AI

13 CLIMATE ACTION

Work in groups to do these activities.

- Make posters on the topic 'Save Trees'. Put them all over your school to create awareness.
- At the end of the year, remove the unused pages of the exercise books. Punch them together and make a 'Busy Book' for yourself.

B. 21 CS Communication | CC Integration with English | HQ Knowing My Needs

15 LIFE ON LAND

Write a story with the title 'Save us and we will save you'.

C. 21 CS Critical Thinking, Life Skills | HQ Coexisting with Nature

12 RESPONSIBLE CONSUMPTION AND PRODUCTION

"Tree can survive without humans but humans cannot survive without trees". Do you agree or disagree? Justify your opinion".

Worksheet 5

STEAM CHALLENGE

One of the major reasons for cutting down a large number of trees is for manufacturing paper. Recycling old paper can save trees. How about making handmade sheets and craft items made from Papier-mâché?

Go, use your creativity and craft some interesting items from Papier-mâché!

What is the challenge?

What supplies do you need?

IDEA 1

IDEA 2

What worked or did not work for you?

How can you improve it?

Review Corner

Review 1 (Chapters 1–2) (Maximum Marks = 25)

A. Choose the correct option. **(1 × 5 = 5)**

1. The decayed bodies of animals mix with the soil to form ____________.
   a. waste b. phosphorus c. humus
2. The food produced by plants is known as ____________.
   a. carbon dioxide b. sugar c. starch
3. ____________ plants shed their leaves in autumn.
   a. Mangrove b. Coniferous c. Deciduous
4. Photosynthesis is carried out in the stem of ____________.
   a. water lily b. cactus c. neem
5. ____________ is an emergent plant.
   a. Tape grass b. Bulrush c. Coralroot

B. Give reasons for the following. **(2 × 2 = 4)**

1. Anita says that a sapling is too young and it cannot make any food. Her friend Rhea says it can make food. Why do you think Rhea says so?
2. Mangroves have special features called breathing roots. Why?

C. Answer these questions. **(3 × 4 = 12)**

1. What will happen if the number of animals suddenly increases on the Earth?
2. How are plants classified according to their habitats?
3. How is a saprophytic plant different from a parasitic plant? Give an example of each.
4. Give two features of a floating plant.

D. Label the diagram. **(1 × 4 = 4)**

Review 2 (Chapters 3–4) (Maximum Marks = 25)

A. Choose the correct option. (1 × 5 = 5)

1. The dark spot in an egg is called ____________.
   a. albumen b. embryo c. egg yolk
2. Another name for a larva is ____________.
   a. caterpillar b. cocoon c. spawn
3. Which of the following gives birth to the young ones and produces milk?
   a. Kiwi b. Whale c. Frog
4. All insects have ____________.
   a. two wings b. six legs c. scales
5. A butterfly has ____________ stages in its life cycle.
   a. three b. four c. five

B. Fill in the blanks. (1 × 4 = 4)

1. ____________ can live on land and in water.
2. An insect's body has a hard-outer covering called ____________.
3. An animal that has blubber is ____________.
4. ____________ is when the bird comes out of the egg shell.

C. Answer these questions. (3 × 4 = 12)

1. What makes kangaroo a mammal? Give three features.
2. Differentiate between hibernation and aestivation.
3. Write any three features that help a penguin to survive in the cold climate.
4. Describe the structure of an egg with the help of a diagram.

D. Label the life cycle of a cockroach. Write one way in which the baby cockroach is similar to the adult cockroach. (3 + 1 = 4)

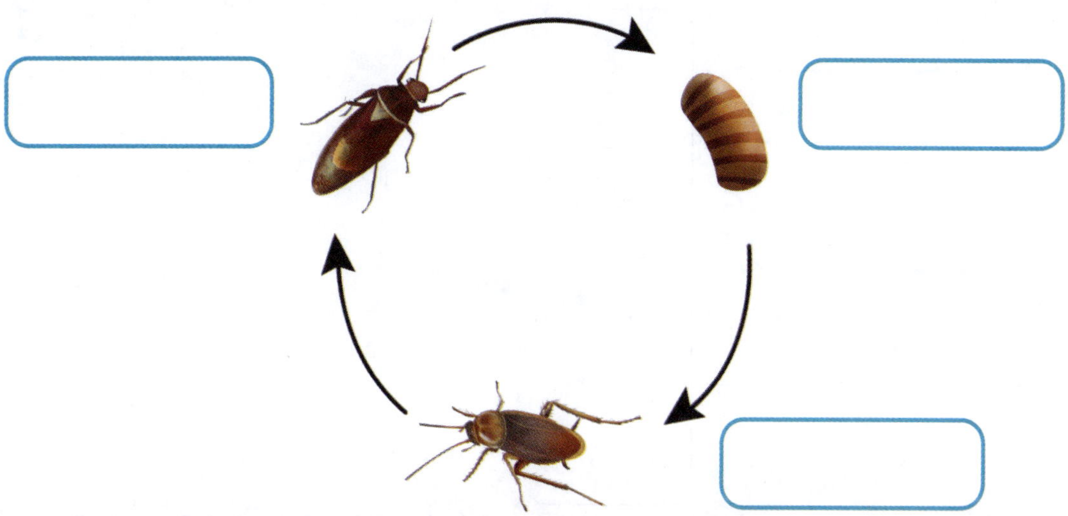

Review 3 (Chapters 5–8) (Maximum Marks = 25)

A. Complete the mind map of the circulatory system. (1 × 6 = 6)

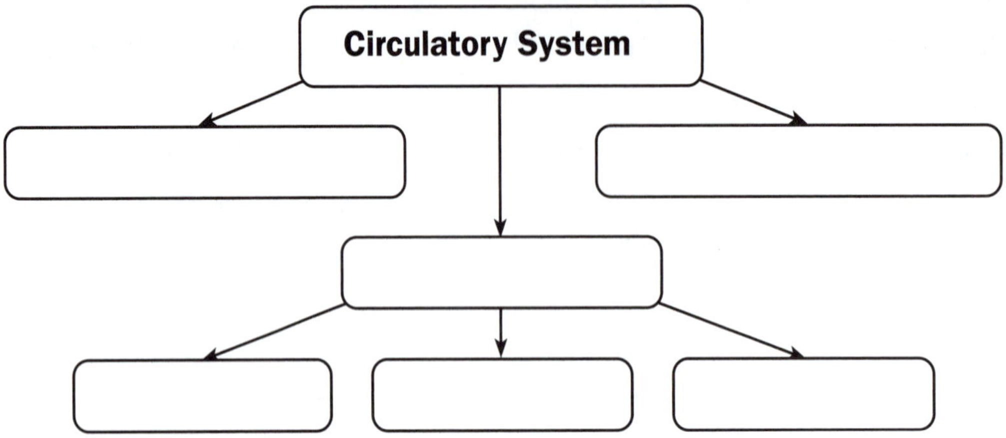

B. Fill in the blanks. (1 × 4 = 4)

1. The hardest part of the human body is ____________________.
2. Fungi that is used in making bread is ____________________.
3. ____________________ is produced by the liver.
4. The process of preventing food from getting spoilt is called ____________________.

C. Answer these questions. (3 × 4 = 12)

1. Name the organs and the functions of the excretory system.
2. What is digestion?
3. Write short notes on bacteria and balanced diet.
4. What are microbes? Describe the four main types of microbes.

D. Label the different parts of a tooth. (1 × 3 = 3)

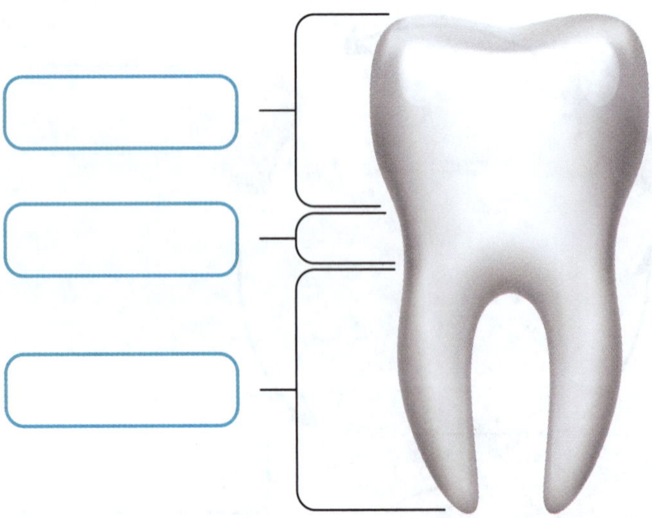

Review 4 (Chapters 9–11) (Maximum Marks = 25)

A. Fill in the blanks. (1 × 5 = 5)

1. The process of breaking down of rocks is called ________________.
2. The process in which a solid or a gas completely dissolves in a liquid is called ________________.
3. Topsoil is rich in ________________.
4. A ________________ is a fossil fuel.
5. The process of water changing into water vapour on heating is called ________________.

B. Name the following. (1 × 5 = 5)

1. The type of simple machine an escalator is ________________
2. Fertile soil that is brought down by rivers ________________
3. Protection of soil from erosion ________________
4. A renewable source of energy ________________
5. Solid that dissolves in water ________________

C. Answer these questions. (3 × 4 = 12)

1. Think of two examples of friction making things we use every day wear out.
2. Explain how matter can change from one state to another.
3. Explain the different sources of energy.
4. Describe the soil profile with the help of a labelled diagram.

D. Look at the pictures and identify the types of machines. (1 × 3 = 3)

Review 5 (Chapters 12–14) **(Maximum Marks = 25)**

A. Choose the correct option. **(1 × 5 = 5)**

1. The heavenly body that moves around a planet in an orbit is a ________.
   a. star b. sun c. satellite
2. World Environment Day is celebrated on ________.
   a. 22nd April b. 5th June c. 26th July
3. The process by which a gas is changed into liquid on cooling is called ________.
   a. melting b. evaporation c. condensation
4. Movement of the Earth around its axis is called ________.
   a. revolution b. rotation c. neither a nor b
5. ________ is a process by which insoluble impurities are separated by passing the water through filters.
   a. Sedimentation b. Filtration c. Decantation

B. Fill in the blanks. **(1 × 5 = 5)**

1. The inner planets are also called ________.
2. The amount of water vapour present in the air is called ________.
3. Planting of trees is called ________.
4. The inner and the outer planets are separated by the ________.
5. ________ is also called the dwarf planet.

C. Answer these questions. **(3 × 4 = 12)**

1. What are the factors that affect evaporation?
2. Describe how we remove soluble impurities from water.
3. Explain how seasons are formed.
4. Write two effects of deforestation.

D. Label the diagram of formation of sea breeze. **(1 × 3 = 3)**

Systems and Cycles

A **system** is made up of two or more parts. These parts work together to do a common function. Systems can be human-made or natural. Plants and animals are examples of natural systems.

The system in our body work together to help us to move, breathe and get energy.

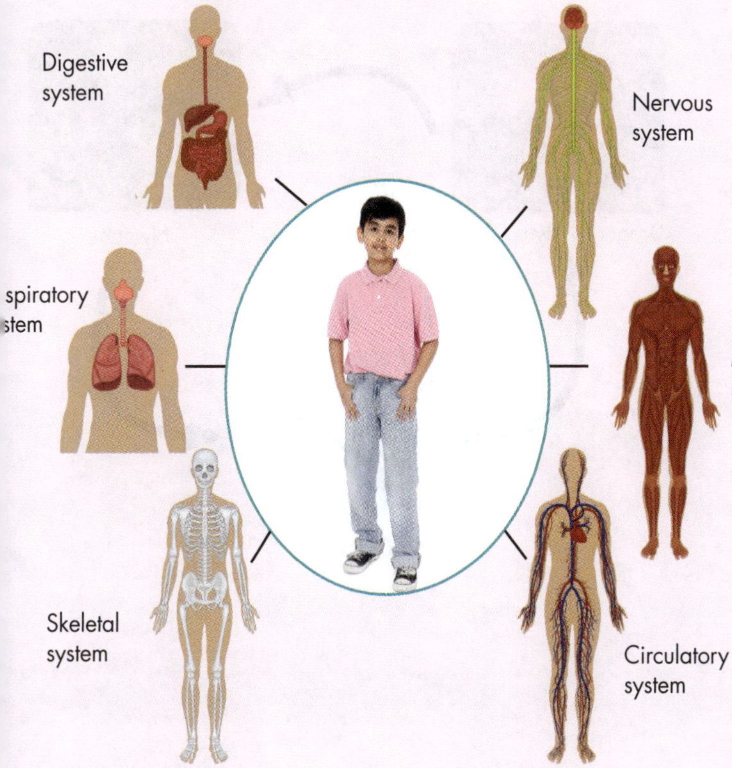

The different parts of a plant work together to keep it healthy and to grow.

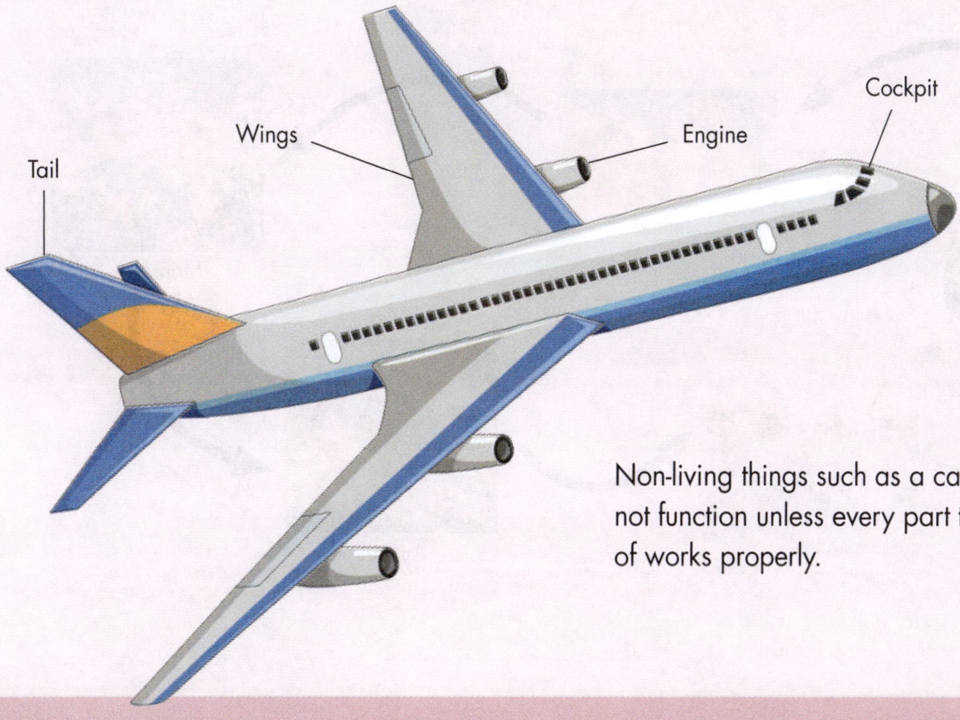

Non-living things such as a car or an aeroplane will not function unless every part that they are made up of works properly.

There are certain patterns of change that repeat themselves in nature. These are called **cycles**.
For example, life cycles of plants and animals. Different cycles take different duration of time to complete.
Some cycles such as change of day to night and night to day happen daily. Change of seasons takes an entire year.
Given below are some important cycles that takes place in the nature.

Life cycle of a **Pea Plant**

Life cycle of a **Dragonfly**

Cycle of **Seasons**

CLASS 4

QUESTION PAPER SET A

NSO

SOF NATIONAL SCIENCE OLYMPIAD 2020-21

DO NOT OPEN THIS BOOKLET UNTIL ASKED TO DO SO

Total Questions: 35 | Time: 1 hr.

Guidelines for the Candidate

1. You will get additional ten minutes to fill up information about yourself on the OMR Sheet, before the start of the exam.
2. Write your **Name, School Code, Class, Section, Roll No.** and **Mobile Number** clearly on the **OMR Sheet** and do not forget to sign it. We will share your marks / result and other information related to SOF exams on your mobile number.
3. The Question Paper comprises three sections:

   Logical Reasoning (5 Questions), **Science** (25 Questions) and **Achievers Section** (5 Questions)

   Each question in Achievers Section carries 2 marks, whereas all other questions carry one mark each.
4. All questions are compulsory. There is no negative marking. Use of calculator is not permitted.
5. There is only ONE correct answer. Choose only ONE option for an answer.
6. To mark your choice of answers by darkening the circles on the OMR Sheet, use **HB Pencil** or **Blue / Black ball point pen** only. E.g.

   Q. 16: Raj goes to school on a bicycle. Which of these safety rules he should follow?

   A. He should give signals before taking turns. B. He should keep to the right of the road.

   C. He should cross the road by using zebra crossing. D. All of these

   As the correct answer is option A, you must darken the circle corresponding to option A on the OMR Sheet. 16. ● Ⓑ Ⓒ Ⓓ
7. Rough work should be done in the blank space provided in the booklet.
8. Return the OMR Sheet to the invigilator at the end of the exam.
9. Please fill in your personal details in the space provided on this page before attempting the paper.

SOF
SCIENCE OLYMPIAD FOUNDATION
Inspiring Young Minds Through Knowledge Olympiads

Name:..

Section:........... SOF Olympiad Roll No.:.. Contact No.:..

1. Select a figure from the options which when placed in the blank space of the given figure would complete the pattern.

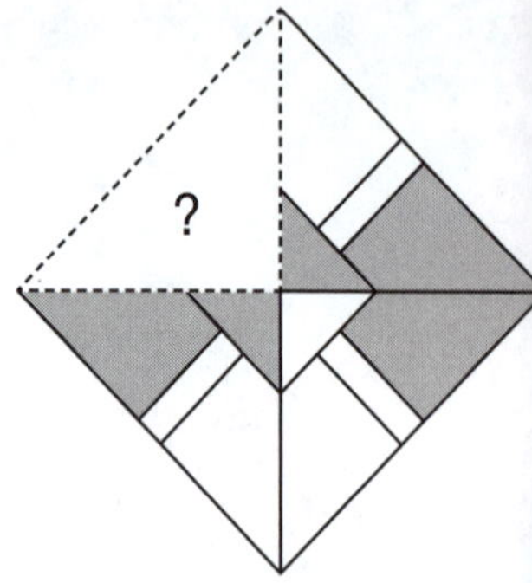

A. 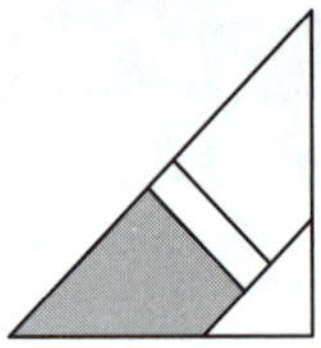

B. 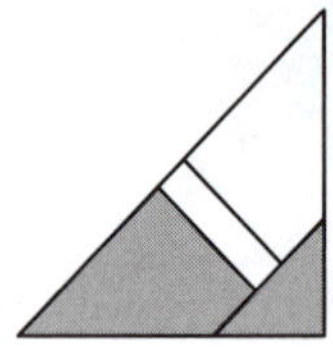

C. 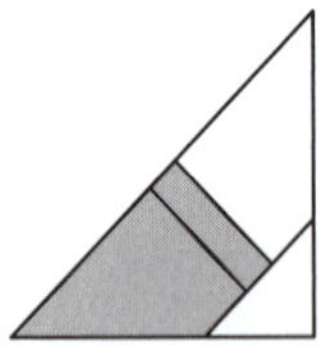

D. 

---

2. In which of the following options, the given figure is exactly embedded as one of its parts?

A. 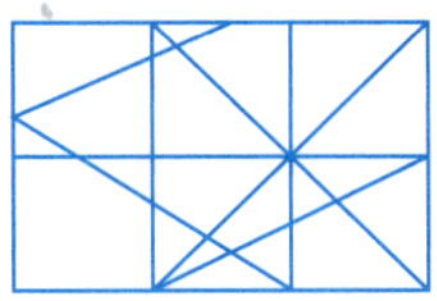

B. 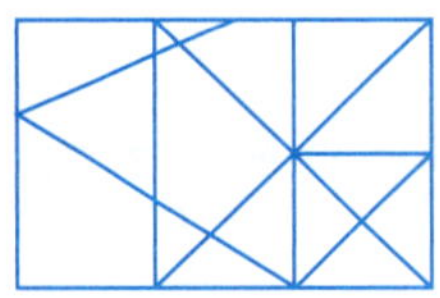

C. 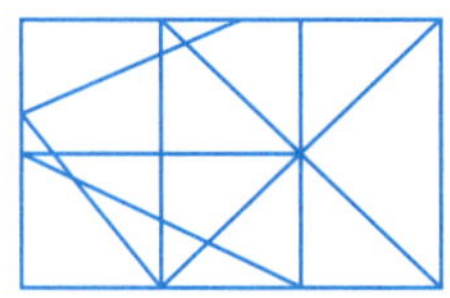

D. 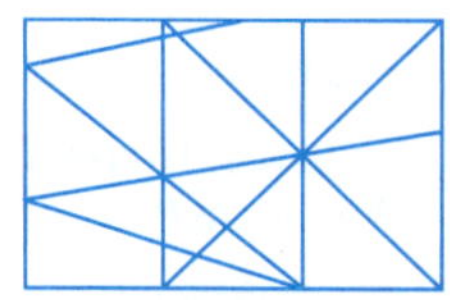

---

3. Find the missing number, if a certain rule is followed either row-wise or column-wise.

8	7	11
9	7	9
5	6	11
77	55	?

A. 90
B 18
C. 75
D. 110

---

4. Who is in the North-East of Ashish?

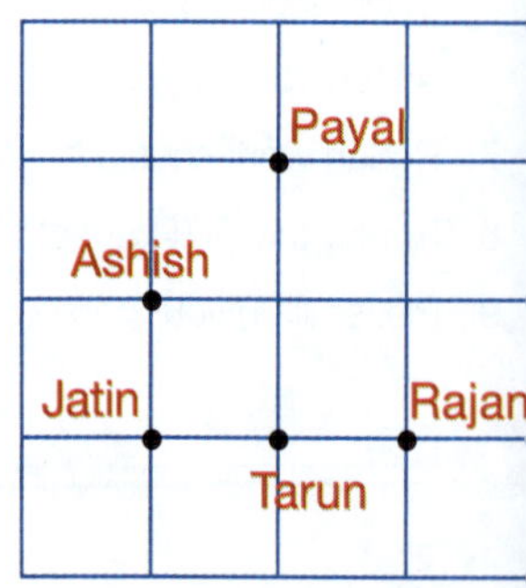

A. Rajan
B. Jatin
C. Payal
D. Tarun

---

5. If 'Grapes' is called 'Mango', 'Mango' is called 'Apple', 'Apple' is called 'Litchi', 'Litchi' is called 'Watermelon' and 'Watermelon' is called 'Orange', then _______ is the heaviest.

A. Orange B. Watermelon C. Litchi D. Mango

SPACE FOR ROUGH WORK

6. Which of the following statements is INCORRECT?
   A. Down feathers of birds keep them warm.
   B. Wading birds have long legs with spread-out toes that help them to walk in water.
   C. Perching birds have two toes in the front and two toes at the back.
   D. Flesh-eating birds such as eagle, vulture and hawk have strong, sharp and hooked beaks.

---

7. Unscramble the given letters to find out the name of a synthetic fibre.
   A. YCCAILR B. NNEIL C. KLSI D. OTCTNO

---

8. Which of the following types of teeth is called tearing tooth?
   A. 
   B. 
   C. 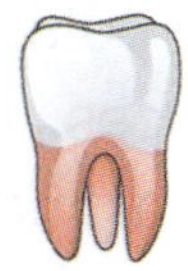
   D. 

---

9. Study the given relationship based on the types of roots these plants possess and select the option that shows similar relationship.

   Bean : Barley : *Hibiscus*

   A. *Eucalyptus* : Banana : Mustard
   B. Rice : Wheat : Maize
   C. Onion : Guava : Beetroot
   D. Turnip : Carrot : Mango

---

10. Which of the following is an INCORRECT statement?
   A. We should not leave toys on the floor after playing.
   B. We should not mop the bathroom floor after taking bath.
   C. We should always swim in the presence of an adult.
   D. We should not consume any medicine on our own.

---

11. A mirror and a glass are placed between a light source and a screen as shown in the given figure.

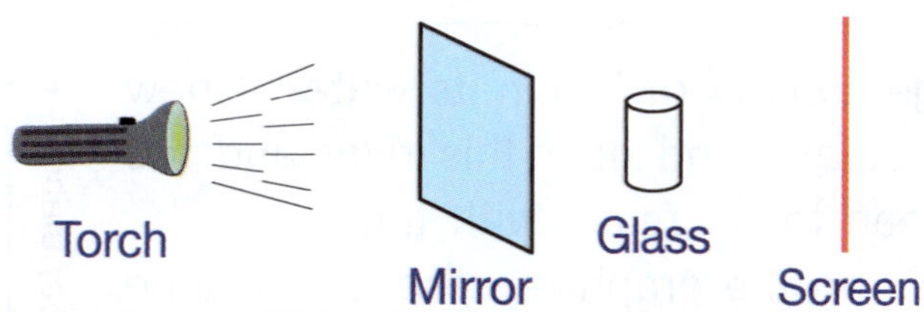

Which of the following shadows will be formed on the screen?

   A. 
   B. 
   C. 
   D. No shadow will be formed

SPACE FOR ROUGH WORK

12. In which of the following rooms of a house the boy shown in the picture must be present?

A. Kitchen
B. Living room
C. Study room
D. Bathroom

---

13. Starting from the first letter strike out every alternate letter to get the name of a professional and select the correct statement regarding it.

PCEOLBMBNLRESRQ

A. He supervises and maintains construction projects, *e.g.,* roads, bridges, etc.
B. He uses wet clay to make pots, vases, *diyas*, etc.
C. He mends old and torn shoes.
D. He treats sick and injured animals.

---

14. Animal shown here is adapted to live at very cold places because it has ___________.

A. Capacity to store water in stomach
B. Flippers for swimming
C. Gills to breathe
D. Layer of fat under skin

---

15. Sakshi and her friends were walking down the road to reach a park. Suddenly, her friend Meeta fell down and got injured.
Which of the following road symbols will help Sakshi to locate the place where Meeta should be taken to?

A. 
B. 
C. 
D. 

---

16. A river supports a large number of fish in its water. A new chemical factory was established near this river and the fish population was seen to decrease with time.
Which point (P, Q or R) on the graph represents the time when factory was established?

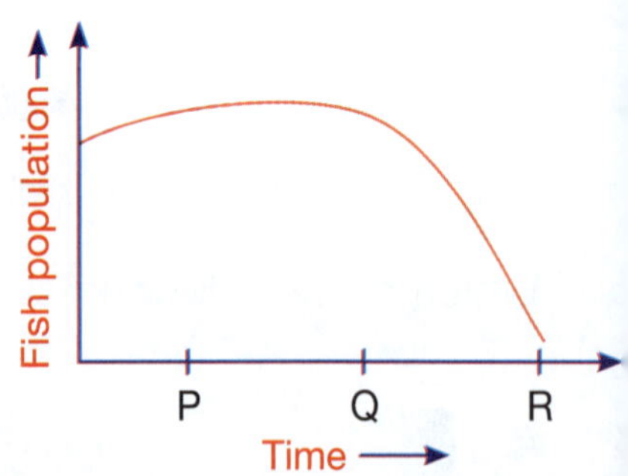

A. P
B. Q
C. R
D. Either Q or R

---

17. Rohit loves to eat chocolates and his mouth starts watering even on seeing chocolates. What is this water in the mouth called?
A. Acid
B. Saliva
C. Mucus
D. Tissue

SPACE FOR ROUGH WORK

18. Kunika took a green leaf. She bleached and washed it in cold water. Then she added a few drops of iodine on it. What will she observe?
   A. The leaf turns pink.
   B. The leaf turns yellow.
   C. The leaf turns blue-black.
   D. The leaf turns red.

---

19. The given diagrams show the shapes of the Moon on different nights.

8th January   15th January

Which one of the following diagrams shows the correct shape of the Moon on 22nd January?

A.  B.  C. 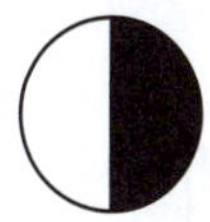 D. 

---

20. Study the given food web and select the correct statements regarding it.

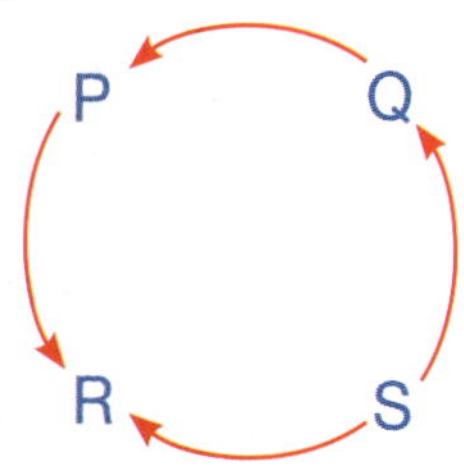

   (i) Q is the food producer.
   (ii) R is both plant and animal eater.
   (iii) R is eaten by P.
   (iv) Q is eaten by P.
   (v) S is an animal eater.

   A. (i) and (v) only B. (ii), (iii) and (iv) only C. (ii) and (iv) only D. (i), (iii) and (v) only

---

21. The Earth takes ________ day(s) to complete one rotation on its axis and _______ day(s) to complete one revolution in its orbit around the Sun.
   A. 28, 365 B. 24, 1 C. 1, 365 D. 24, 365

---

22. Select the option that correctly identifies X.

X
It allows light to pass through it.
It has a fixed shape.
It has a fixed volume.

   A. Marble tile
   B. Glass
   C. Water
   D. Carbon dioxide

---

23. ________ is the organ where absorption of water from undigested food occurs.

A. 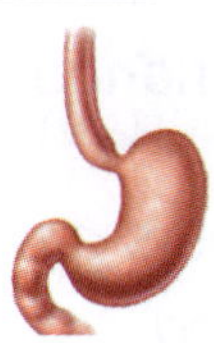 B. 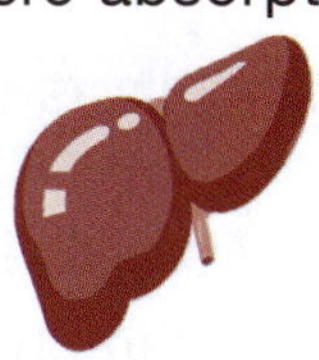 C.  D. 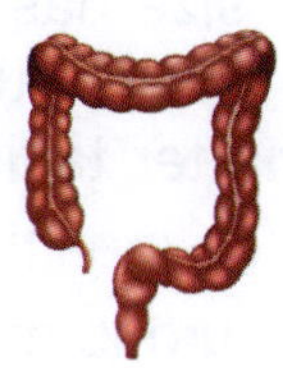

SPACE FOR ROUGH WORK

24. Study the given classification chart.

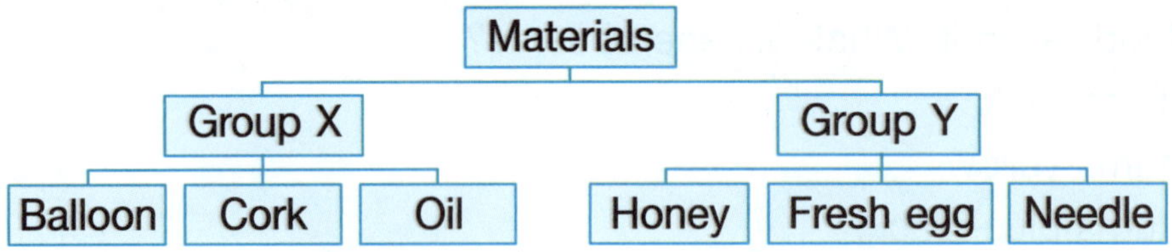

Which of the following are the most suitable headings for the groups X and Y?

	Group X	**Group Y**		**Group X**	**Group Y**
A.	Translucent	Opaque	B.	Hard	Soft
C.	Float on water	Sink in water	D.	Natural	Man-made

---

25. Rupali plotted a graph to show the intensity of sound heard during the activities X, Y and Z. Which of the following graphs would she have obtained?

Key:
X → Sound made by a cricket
Y → Jet plane taking off
Z → Alarm clock ringing in a vacuum

A. 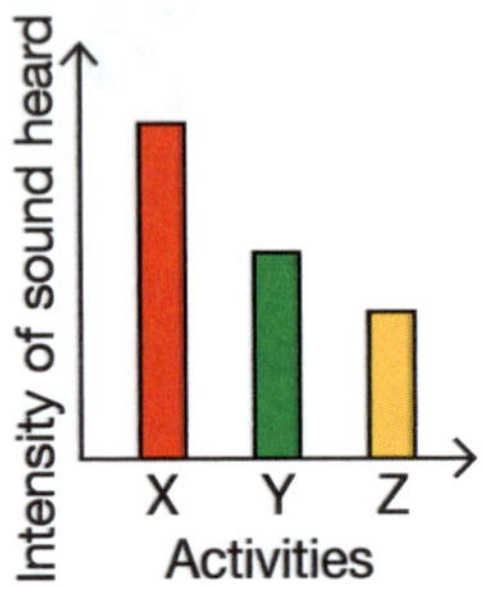

B. 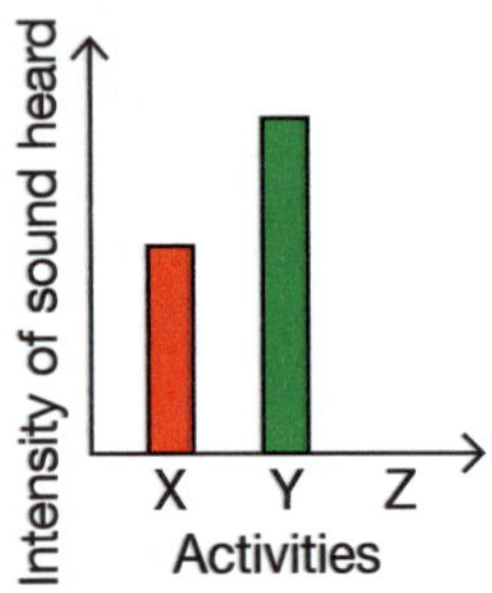

C. 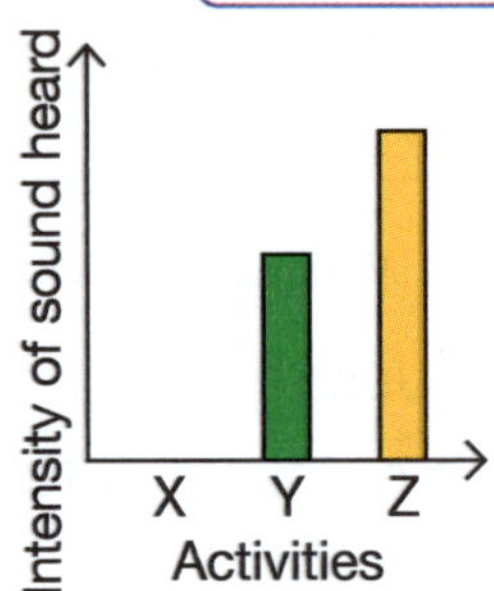

D. 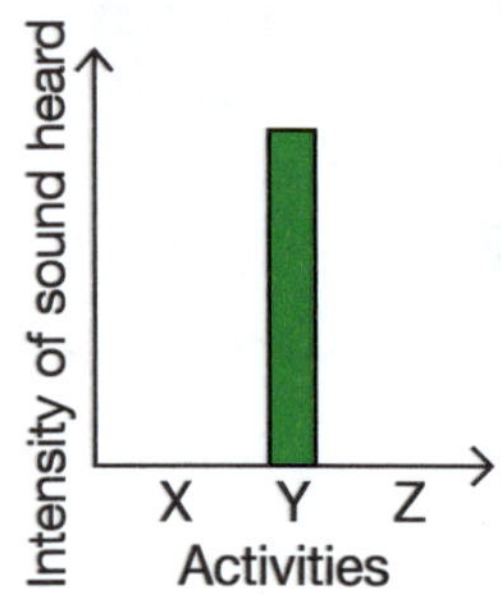

---

26. The given table shows the time taken by a ball to roll over the same distance over four different surfaces P, Q, R and S.

If the ball is pushed with the same force in each case, then which surface P, Q, R or S is the smoothest?

Surface	Time taken by ball
P	6 seconds
Q	15 seconds
R	10 seconds
S	18 seconds

A. P
B. R
C. S
D. Q

---

27. Identify 'it' in the given riddle.

It normally grows in fields.
It is a grain from what I hear.
It can be eaten piece by piece
Or straight from a long ear.

A. Banana
B. Lemon
C. Corn
D. Onion

---

28. Rubina kept some naphthalene balls in her almirah. After few days, she observed that their size has decreased.
The change that occurred in size of naphthalene balls is similar to the change in state of matter taking place when ________.

A. Ice-cream is put on a table
B. Water is boiled and vapours are formed
C. Curd is made from milk
D. A camphor block is heated

SPACE FOR ROUGH WORK

29. Study the given figure of water cycle. Which of the given processes is also responsible for our foggy breath in winters?

A. P

B. R

C. Q

D. Either Q or R

---

30. Study the given classification table formed on the basis of method of cooking and identify P and Q.

Group X	Group Y
Momos	*Samosa*
Dhokla	Q
P	*Pakora*

	P	**Q**
A.	Cake	Jam
B.	Pickle	Biscuit
C.	Eggs	Rice
D.	*Idli*	*Poori*

ACHIEVERS SECTION

31. Match column I with column II and select the correct option from the codes given below.

Column I	**Column II**
a. Inclined plane	(i) Bottle opener
b. Wheel and axle	(ii) Ramp
c. Lever	(iii) Jar lid
d. Screw	(iv) Screwdriver
e. Wedge	(v) Fork

	a	**b**	**c**	**d**	**e**
A.	(iii)	(ii)	(iv)	(v)	(i)
B.	(i)	(iii)	(v)	(iv)	(ii)
C.	(iv)	(v)	(iii)	(ii)	(i)
D.	(ii)	(iv)	(i)	(iii)	(v)

---

32. Read the given statements and select the option that correctly identifies them as true(T) and false (F) ones.

(i) Copper and gold are ductile materials.

(ii) Winnowing is used to separate grains from stalks by beating them.

(iii) Generally solubility of gases decreases with increase in temperature.

(iv) Oxygen gas is insoluble in water.

	(i)	**(ii)**	**(iii)**	**(iv)**
A.	T	T	F	F
B.	F	F	F	T
C.	T	F	T	F
D.	F	T	F	T

33. Which of the following statements is correct regarding sea breeze?

(i) Hot air blows from sea towards land.
(ii) Hot air on the land rises up.
(iii) Cool air blows from land towards sea.
(iv) Cool air on the sea rises up.

A. (i) only
B. (ii) only
C. (ii) and (iii) only
D. (i), (iii) and (iv) only

34. Study the given Venn diagram.

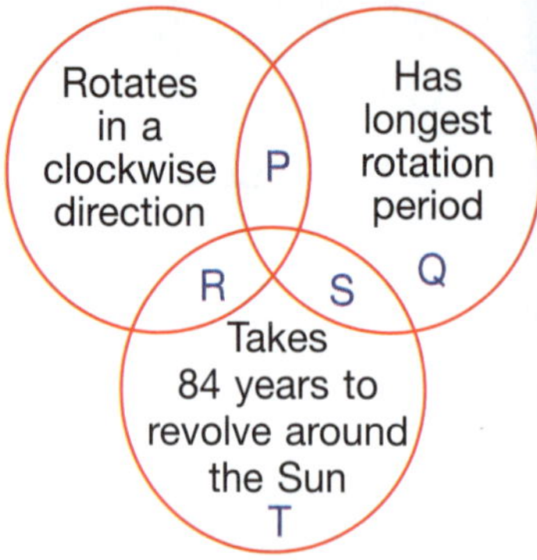

Which letters (P–T) represent Venus and Uranus?

	Venus	**Uranus**
A.	Q	R
B.	T	S
C.	P	R
D.	R	S

35. Study the given flow chart and select the INCORRECT option.

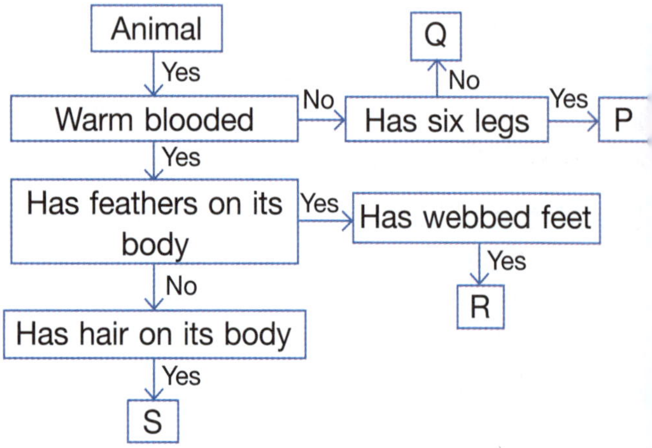

A. Q can be an animal with gills to breathe.
B. P can be an animal from whose cocoon silk is obtained.
C. S can be an animal that carries its young one in a pouch.
D. R can be an animal whose nest is called eyrie.

National Office: Plot 99, First Floor, Sector 44 Institutional area, Gurugram -122 003 (HR) India
Email: info@sofworld.org | Website: www.sofworld.org
Regd. Office: 406, Taj Apt., Ring Road, New Delhi-110 029
Note: Please address all communication to the National Office only.

KEYWORDS

Chapter 1

Lamina: flat part of the leaf

Petiole: part of the plant that attaches the leaf to the stem

Midrib: the tube-like structure that runs through the middle of the leaf

Stomata: the tiny pores found mainly on the underside of the leaf

Photosynthesis: a process by which green plants make their own food

Chapter 2

Habitat: the place in nature where a living thing lives

Adaptation: a special feature that helps a living thing to adjust and live in its habitat

Terrestrial plants: plants that grow on land

Deciduous trees: trees that shed their leaves

Evergreen trees: trees that do not shed their leaves

Aquatic plants: plants that grow in water

Emergent plants: plants that have their roots in the waterbed but leaves and stems extend above the water surface

Saprophytic plants: plants that get their nutrition from dead or decaying matters

Parasitic plants: plants that live on other plants to get nutrition

Carnivorous plants: plants that trap and digest insects

Breathing roots: roots that grow above the ground in swampy areas

Chapter 3

Reproduction: the process by which animals produce young ones of their own kind

Mammals: animals that give birth to their young ones

Life cycle: the stages of development of a living thing from beginning to the end of life

Hatching: when the baby bird breaks the egg shell to come out

Embryo: the dark spot in the egg yolk that is actually the developing baby

Albumen: the white watery substance that lies just outside the yolk

Metamorphosis: the process of changing of a young one into a completely different looking adult

Chapter 4

Adaptation: features that help living things to survive in their habitat

Vertebrates: animals with backbone

Invertebrates: animals without backbone

Exoskeleton: hard outer covering of an insect's body

Aerial animals: animals that fly and spend a lot of time in the air

Arboreal animals: land animals that live mostly on trees

Hibernation: the long sleep of some animals during winter

Aestivation: the long sleep of some animals during summer

Parasites: animals that draw their nutrition from other animals

Camouflage: shape and colour of an animal that help them to merge with the environment

Extinct: animals that have disappeared from the Earth

Endangered: animals that are in the danger of disappearing from the Earth

Chapter 5

Nutrients: substances present in food necessary for growth

Roughage: fibres in food, which cannot be digested but help in getting rid of wastes from the body

Balanced diet: a diet that has all the nutrients in the right proportion

Preservation: the process of preventing food from getting spoilt

Preservatives: certain chemicals that are added to food to prevent it from getting spoilt

Chapter 6

Enamel: the outermost covering of the tooth that is the hardest substance in human body

Dentine: lies just below the enamel but is not as hard as enamel

Pulp: soft part of the tooth that has nerves and blood vessels

Incisors: front teeth that help us to bite and cut

Canines: sharp, pointed teeth found next to the incisors

Premolars: flat, broad teeth that help in chewing, grinding and crushing

Molars: teeth broader than premolars that help in chewing, grinding and crushing

Microbes: tiny living organisms that can be seen only with the help of a microscope

Chapter 7

Digestion: breaking food into smaller particles that can be easily absorbed by the body

Digestive system: mouth, food pipe, stomach, liver, pancreas, small intestine, large intestine and anus form the digestive system

Chapter 8

Circulatory system: organ system formed by the heart, blood and blood vessels

Heart: a muscular organ that pumps blood

Blood vessels: thin tube-like structures that carry blood

Arteries: blood vessels that carry blood from the heart to other parts of the body

Veins: blood vessels that carry blood from different parts of the body to the heart

Capillaries: the smallest blood vessels where exchange of nutrients, oxygen, carbon dioxide and water takes place

Excretory system: organ system that helps to get rid of the waste from the body

Chapter 9

Weathering: the process of breaking down of rocks

Topsoil: uppermost layer of soil

Humus: the remains of dead plants and animals in the soil

Subsoil: the middle layer of soil

Bedrock: the bottom most layer of soil

Soil erosion: the wearing away of topsoil by the action of wind, rain or human activity

Soil conservation: prevention of topsoil from erosion

Crop rotation: growing different kinds of crops in the same field in different Seasons

Chapter 10

Matter: anything that has mass and occupies space

Volume: amount of space that matter occupies

Intermolecular space: space between two molecules

Solute: a solid that dissolves in a liquid

Solvent: a liquid in which a solid dissolves

Solution: the liquid that we get when a solid dissolves in a liquid

Chapter 11

Force: a pull or push

Gravity: a force that pulls everything towards the Earth

Friction: force that acts when two surfaces move or slide against one another

Muscular force: force applied by the muscles

Mechanical force: force produced by machines

Magnetic force: force exerted by a magnet

Fossil fuel: fuels formed from the dead remains of plants and animals that died millions of years ago

Chapter 12

Weather: condition of the atmosphere of a place at a particular time

Atmosphere: blanket of air around the Earth

Sea breeze: wind that blows during the day from sea to land

Land breeze: wind that blows at night from land to sea

Water cycle: process where water is constantly moving in a cycle from the surface of the Earth to the sky and then back to the ground

Humidity: amount of water vapour in the air

Freezing: changing of water into ice on cooling

Precipitation: rain, snow and hail that fall to the ground

Sedimentation: process of purifying water so that the heavy impurities settle down at the bottom of the container

Decantation: pouring of clear water, obtained after sedimentation, which is on top of the container

Filtration: process in which insoluble impurities are separated by passing the water through filters

Chapter 13

Planets: heavenly bodies that revolve around the sun

Satellite: an object that revolves around a planet

Axis: vertical imaginary line passing through the centre of the Earth, running from North Pole to South Pole

Rotation: movement of the Earth on its own axis

Revolution: movement of the Earth around the sun

Chapter 14

Deforestation: cutting down of trees in large numbers

Afforestation: planting of trees

Fibres and Fabrics

Rani, this is a jute stall. Jute is a long, shiny, vegetable fibre obtained from the jute plant that can be spun into a coarse strong thread. When the stems are ready to cut, they are soaked in water. The fibres are then removed from the stalk, spun into a yarn and finally made into jute bags, ropes, sacks, mats and some clothes. Now, I will take you to the silk stall.
Jute
Silk is a lustrous fibre that is obtained from silkworms. Hundreds of eggs are laid by the silk moths. Caterpillars hatch and eat greedily and grow fat. Then they build a cocoon around them. Threads are then pulled out from the cocoons, reeled and made into silk cloth. Silk cloth is used to design sarees, dress materials etc.
Silk
Mom, can you take me to the woollen stall also?
Rani, this is a woollen stall. Sheep are reared for their fleece which is made into wool. The fleece is first sheared, which is followed by scouring (removing dirt, dust, grease), washing, separating into different fibres, then straightening and rolling into the yarn. The fine wool fibre yarn is dyed for knitting into pullovers, jerseys and the coarse fibre is used for making carpets.
Woollen

Synthetic Fibres
Mom, what are synthetic fibres?
Rani, the fibres that do not occur naturally and are made by human beings are called synthetic or human-made fibres. Rayon, nylon and polyester are some of its examples. As fibres, these materials are known for their strength, toughness, resistance to heat and ability to hold a pressed form.

Fibre Fair
Rani, did you like the fair? Would you be able to complete your project now?
Yes mom, I learnt a lot about fibres today. I think, I will be able to complete my project.

21 CS Critical Thinking, Life Skills | HQ Coexisting with Nature

SEE Learning (Social Emotional Ethical)

A Friend in Need is a Friend Indeed!

3 GOOD HEALTH AND WELL-BEING

My SEE Social Emotional Ethical Space

A. What do you think caused Granny's bad cough and fever?

____

____

B. Can you name at least two diseases that are caused by virus or other microbes?

____

____

C. Think of an incident where you helped a friend or a friend helped you. How did you feel about that? Share your thoughts in the space given below.

____

____

____

____

D. Do you have a picture of yourself with your friends? Paste the picture in the space given below or make a sketch of yourself with your friends.

Science Fair: Make a Seesaw

A **seesaw** or **teeter-totter** found in a playground is actually a simple machine called lever.

All You Need Is... Paper straws, thick piece of paper, paper cups, glue and small toys to put in the seesaw chairs

Let's Start!

1 Take nine straw pieces 4 cm each. With the help of glue, fix the straw pieces to make the seesaw base.

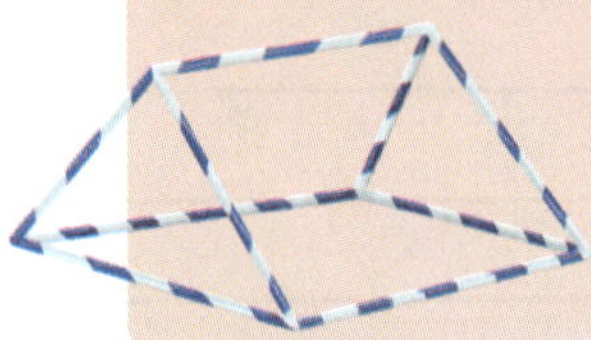

2 Take a 3 cm wide piece of paper and roll it over the top of the seesaw base to make a freely moving ring. Fix the free end of the paper with glue.

3 Take six 15 cm long straight paper straws. Fix them on a small thick piece of paper to make the arm of the seesaw.

4 Take two paper cups and cut them to make two chairs. Fix the chairs to the two ends of the seesaw arm.

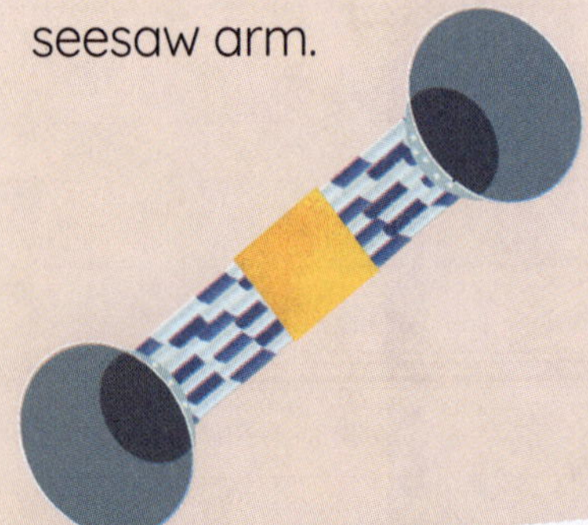

5 Fix the centre of the seesaw arm to the ring on the seesaw base.

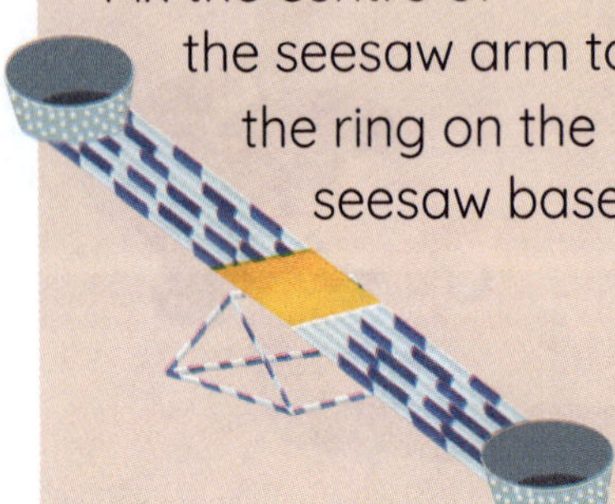

6 Your seesaw is ready. Place your favourite toys on it and have fun!

***Note:** Do not use scissors by yourself. Take the help of an elder.*

Do It Yourself!

Find out the various uses of a pulley and write in the space given below.

____

____

____

____

____

____

____

Pulley is a simple machine that uses a wheel with a rope to lift heavy objects.

Make a working model of an equipment from real life that uses a pulley. Write the materials required and the steps of its construction. Make the diagram or paste a picture of your model in the space given below.

All I Need Is: ____

____

____

____

Let's Start: ____

____

____

____

____

____

____

____

____

____

____

____

Eminent Scientists

21 CS Information Literacy

IF

5 GENDER EQUALITY

Dr Vikram Sarabhai (1919–1971)

Dr Sarabhai was an Indian physicist and astronomer. He started space research and helped in developing nuclear power in India. For his contributions, he was honoured with Padma Bhushan and Padma Vibhushan. He is called the 'Father of the Indian space program'.

Marie Curie (1867–1934)

Marie Curie was a Polish-born French scientist who won two Nobel prizes. She conducted pioneering research on radioactivity. She was the first woman to get a Nobel Prize. Not only this, she was the first and the only woman to win the Nobel Prize twice in two scientific fields, that is, chemistry and physics.

Charaka (approximately between 200 BCE–200 CE)

Charaka is considered to be the first Indian physician. He was one of the principal contributors to Ayurveda, a system of medicine and lifestyle developed in ancient India. Charak is referred as the 'Father of medicine'. His work on Charak Samhita is considered an encyclopedia of Ayurveda.